STRAIGHT UP!

Teens' Guide to Taking Charge of Their Lives

A Sourcebook for Teens and Parents
2nd Edition

STRAIGHT UP!

Teens' Guide to Taking Charge of Their Lives

A Sourcebook for Teens and Parents
2nd Edition

Dr. Elizabeth D. Taylor
With Tracey L. Taylor

STRAIGHT UP! Teens' Guide to Taking Charge of Their Lives
Second Edition

By Dr. Elizabeth D. Taylor
With Tracey Leroy Taylor

Published by:
Wisdom To Go Alliance
P.O. Box 91473
Phoenix, AZ 85066-1473
Phone: 602-243-9882
Email: etaylor@wisdomtogo.com

Dr. Elizabeth D. Taylor, Publisher and Editorial Director
Yvonne Rose/Quality Press – Project Consultant/Coordinator
The Printed Page, Interior Design/Back Cover Layout

ISBN 10: 0-9778466-0-1
ISBN 13: 978-0-9778466-0-3

Dedicated to
Julian-Sebastian

With eternal gratitude of
Gloria Louise Taylor

In loving memory of
Albade and Obadiah Taylor

Artistic Credits:

Front Cover Art, Dion James
Back Cover Art, Sonia Gutierrez
Cover and Photos Layout, Greer Ashman

(Dion and Sonia are in the class of 2008 at South Mountain High School in Phoenix, Arizona. They are students in Sebastio Pereira's Advanced Drawing & Painting, Visual Arts Magnet.)

Interior Graphics ("In the Spirit", "Parenting Pie" and Chapter 7 imaging), by Greer Ashman

Photography for "You Got Game" and "What You Can Do" courtesy of Star Shine Academy

Photography for Dr. Taylor's Bio, courtesy of Chau Nguyen

Other chapter photography courtesy of Elizabeth Taylor, the Morris family, Cheryl LaJoye, Terence Brown and Britaneé Perkins

Acknowledgments

*I thank and remember Ruth Steiner
for her tremendous generosity and faith in this work,
in all ways and from the very beginning.*

*I gratefully acknowledge the St. Luke's Health Initiative
in Phoenix Arizona,
for their generous and enthusiastic contribution
to make this book possible.*

*I thank Dr. Ward Ashman for providing the energy and
resources to make the writing of this book
a joyful and fulfilling experience.*

*Thank you Donna Beasley for your insight and will to
launch this pioneering guidebook for teens in 1994.*

*Thanks to the countless others who helped to make
this 2nd edition come to life.*

*And
Kudos to our Straight Up! youth for your inspiring images
in this book: Amber, Anabel, Anna, Britaneé, Dion, Drew,
Frank, Grayson, Gregory, Jalil, Jared, Julian-Sebastian,
Marcella, Samantha, Stephen, Taylor and Terence!*

If you would like to join our contributors by supporting *Straight Up!*
youth projects, please email or contact us at: www.wisdomtogo.com or
Wisdom To Go, Inc. P.O, Box 91473, Phoenix, Arizona 85066-1473.

About This Book

Late one evening in January 1996, I received a call from a colleague. She said to me *"Dr. Taylor, I just called to tell you that today, a friend of mine was evicted from her home with her two grandchildren. One of the grandchildren, a teenage girl, came to my home tonight, a few hours ago, needing a place to stay. I noticed that the only thing she brought was a small backpack containing the few things she had time to collect from her grandmother's home. I put the young woman to bed, and was lifting her backpack from the floor when a book fell out. The book was the one you wrote. It was called **Straight Up!**"*

In November 2002 my nephew Gregory called me from Texas where he had been attending Texas Southern University. He said: *"Auntie, you will not believe what just happened today!"* What happened darlin? *"I walked into a Child Development class on campus to speak with the teacher, and saw that he was reading from a book that looked like yours. I told the teacher and the students that that was my aunt's book! He thought I was joking and tried to dismiss me, claiming that it wasn't. So I asked him to hand me the book. I opened it to the page where my name is mentioned in the Dedication. And then he knew that I was telling the truth."*

There are many other such stories attached to **Straight Up!** which speak to its magic and power. I share these stories with you to illustrate the depth at which **Straight Up!** touches young lives. This makes me proud and blessed.

Straight Up! was originally published in 1994 by Lindsay Publishing in Chicago, Illinois. It was a pioneering book, the first of its kind—a lifeskills book for African-American teens, with an emphasis on spiritual development.

Although it was doubted by cynics that teens would read it, let alone African-American teens, the book to the contrary, was read by African-American teens, teens from other races, as well as parents and educators. It has reached young people both, nationally and internationally. It has been referenced in youth workshops, youth centers, and ministries across the country, and featured on national radio and TV talk shows. *Straight Up!* went on to win the *1996 National Library Association Award—Quick Picks for Teens.*

The ongoing demand for **Straight Up!** makes it clear that the need remains strong for a book of this kind; and that this little book has and continues to do its job. This new 2nd Edition is expanded, fortified and just as spirited. It is written for a broader population of young people from all ethnic backgrounds and walks of life, as well as the parents and adults who care for and about them. I have poured so much more of my heart into this 2nd Edition, and experienced the re-writing of **Straight Up!** as a jewel of an odyssey.

Because youth are 40% of today's population and 100% of our future **Straight Up!** remains dedicated to helping young people be the best that they can be.

This revised edition of **Straight Up!** is a proud publication of Wisdom To Go, Inc.

—*Dr. Elizabeth D. Taylor*

Foreword—*Fade In*

You are an aware and intelligent teenager. Why? For one reason, you have chosen to pick up and read this book. You are facing a bold and wonder filled world. You may be asking questions. Where will you go and how far? Whom can you trust and who is there for you? Do you have what it takes? Will people hear about you, and for what reasons? You may be wondering, "Who am I?" If you are perplexed by these kinds of questions you have began the process of finding some answers here. You are in the right place. From here you can begin to go *Straight Up!*

The answers to your questions begin with these simple facts of life:
1. You are to enjoy your life, to experience abundance and success.

2. You have a responsibility to do your best.

3. You are here to make a positive contribution to life on the planet.

Yes, I know, it's not that simple. There is the *real world* that you must deal with. Let's go there and get back to this.

When I talk with teens like you, they share many concerns about the challenges they face today: Sex, drugs, peer pressure, family problems, low self-esteem, self-doubt, identity, support, depression, anger and hopelessness. They have many questions about race and culture, about violence, and the decay and corruption they see in our social institutions. Like you, they are wondering who are they becoming, and what kind of world are they stepping into. So you see, you are not alone. These things are not to be taken lightly. They represent potential roadblocks and barriers that can and will stop you dead in your tracks on your journey.

BUT, by reaching for this little book, that outcome is less likely to occur.

So back to those three facts of your life: As a modern teen, you have a different experience than the generation of your parents and teachers. You have a greater opportunity to be more aware, more inquiring and to make more powerful choices. Why? Because this is the nature of the times in which you live. This is both a blessing and a curse, because when more is there for you more is expected of you. Your life requires alternative and strong medicine for the challenges you face and will continue to encounter. It will require a broader scope and perspective to embrace all that is possible for you. You have the capacity to grasp deep profound truths—to look beyond that which is shallow and superficial. You have the capacity to go beyond race, culture, economic status or social conditioning. In fact, deep down inside, you want and need to do this. Yours is a culture of boundless energy, of light, creativity and boldness! And where there is boldness there is magic. Your free will and responsible choice is the magic wand you use to create the life your heart desires!

So choose and choose wisely!

How To Read This Book

A 'tool' is wisdom or an approach that you apply to a problem, concern or situation. *Straight Up!* is your personal 'toolbox' for being who you want to be and creating the life you want. This little book is now your friend. Make it your encyclopedia for personal growth in a dynamic and demanding world. Read *Straight Up!* regularly, thoughtfully, and thoroughly. If you don't understand something, leave it, read on and come back to it. This is a book that will grow with you. Come to it with your problems. Seek it out for encouragement and inspiration. Listen to it. Take your time. Take it in small doses. Share it with a parent, counselor, teacher or mentor. Share it with a friend. And after reading *Straight Up!* once, read it again. Keep it as a permanent part of your personal library. Grow with it. And pass it on. *Straight Up!'s* message is timeless, relevant and vital to your life today and tomorrow.

Chapters 1 and 2 lay out the basics of teen life today and speak to your questions about your place in the greater scheme of things. These chapters set you up with a perspective on spirituality that is essential to you. *Chapter 3* talks about the downs and ups of family life and relationships, and how you can ride those waves. *Chapter 4* describes the "real world" you are entering and how to navigate your way through worldly obstacles and into opportunities. In *Chapter 5* you will learn about your inner world of thoughts and beliefs, and how you can manage this world by overcoming negative emotions, beliefs and programming.

A book for teens cannot be authentic without some reference to parenting. *Chapter 6* is provided to put parents and teens on the "same page"—to help parents help you. This is also done to foster partnerships between parents and teens that can help you be the best you can be. *Chapter 7* tells you about the spiritual laws that affect your life and how you can work with them. A *'What You Can Do'* Quick Reference is provided for those times when all you need is a quick response to a problem or issue. It takes you directly to the life tools and navigational skills you may need on the spot. And an *Appendix* that features "how-to" guides on goal setting, building self-esteem and managing conflict is extra!

InJoy!

Contents

The Game

He got game, she got game
They gave up studying because it's so lame

She was an academic achiever to any school named
too bad she was distracted and has no one to blame

Dude was a scholar and ball player
he had the gift to become a hall of fame player

Universities wanted him across the country
his name was known from county to county

He started to party just a little bit
he started smoking weed just a little bit

He had sex with his girl just a little bit
his grades started to slip just a little bit

His mom and teachers were worried just a bit
his ball playing went down so he had to sit

His girl friend got pregnant with a baby boy
that's so sad because he's unemployed

They're caught in a game they can't play
three lives now infected and the parents just pray

If only they kept their eyes on the prize
they would not choose to ruin their young lives

You want to avoid this real life drama claiming you?
Yo! keep studying and learning before the same game plays you.
—Tracey Taylor

Chapter One

Word is Born!

It's not over until I win!
—Anonymous

Word. Your only real opponent in this life is your self, not the other person or the other team. When all is said and done, you compete and win against your self. And your goal is to win by being and doing your best. With this in mind, know that there are three kinds of people in the world. There are those on the court *workin'* the game. There are those in the stands watching the game. And there are those in the parking lot wondering what is going on.

It's On!

It's the 4th quarter of the basketball finals. Your team didn't cut it last year; now it's neck and neck with the reigning champions. It is game 7 of a heated series, 4.7 seconds on the clock with your team down by 1 point. With no more time-outs, the ball is hurled in your direction. Heavy defense is on your heels and thick in the paint. All eyes are fixed on you, as you, in that short moment, summon up your skill, determination and resolve. It's on!

Do you buckle from the pressure? Does the ball bounce off the rim from a feeble toss? Or do you in that split second, zero in on the target, jam the ball home, and bring the house down?

Focus must be found! The challenges and dynamics of the world today are just as compelling as this peak moment. Unlike those of your parents, they require different responses and coping skills if you want to get ahead. It's the championship game of life, and you can either make your move or foul out. Like the clutch player you must be adept, you must be alert, you must be focused and clear. Because the choices you make right now will impact the remainder of your life.

This is a fabulous time to be alive! The world opening up to you is rich with possibilities. There are so many paths you can take, more than existed 10, even 5 years ago. The opportunities for you are diversifying and increasing at an accelerating pace. Anything you think you can achieve is possible. Yes, you can truly be "all that!" This is true whether you were born with a silver spoon in your mouth, or if you were sent to bed on an empty stomach.

This is also a time when you are highly challenged—both positively and negatively. You are challenged to conduct your self responsibly and to steer clear of temptations that can trip you up, such as sex, drugs, or delinquent behavior. You are challenged to thrive in environments where you may not be supported—where there may be abuse, fear or ignorance. You are challenged to self-motivate and rise above ego and its excesses, such as pride, laziness, greed, anger and hate. You must also deal with the challenge that comes from choosing from a multitude of opportunities and possibilities, and the directions you can go. You have more choices to make on how you are going to live your life, what vocation or career you will pursue, where you will live, what kind of music you will listen to, what kind of people you invite into your circle, and what kind of image and style you will present to the world. You will be challenged to choose wisely in these areas, and more.

With today's possibilities come greater insecurity, and fewer protections and guarantees. There is strong competition, and higher standards to meet—more than your parents faced as teenagers. You must navigate this terrain.

These challenges you face mean that more is expected of you. And because more is expected of you, you can experience pressure. You cannot afford to sit back and wait for someone else to make things work for you, to give you something, or to even make you do something. This is not a time to squander your gift, time, energy or resources. To wait, and hope and put things off places you at risk of losing pace and stagnating as doors to opportunity close, and the world moves on without you. Today, it is easy to lose your balance and fall through the cracks. It is easy to stay stuck doing the same thing. Really, it doesn't take much effort. Just do nothing!

You already have your 'free pass' to participate in life, and that is your birth certificate! Meeting challenges and staying in the game requires no less than your best in the forms of: A *positive attitude, vision, skills, commitment, wisdom* and your free will to make *responsible choices.*

Playing To Win

Good news! You are now free to be all you can be. In fact this is required! The times call upon you to dig deep and use all you've got. There are as many ways to fail, as there are to succeed. These are not times for excuses. The time for blaming and playing the victim is over. No one—of any race, culture or creed, can go very far by pointing a finger and blaming others for their problems, shortcomings or failures. You have many options; failure is not one of them.

Your life is what you make it through your beliefs, thoughts, feelings and choices. These are the colors you use to create the tapestry of your life. Blaming, negativity and idleness lead to dead ends. These are not rewarded in today's teaming world landscape. Self-initiative, integrity, positivity and responsibility are. Today people are less likely to identify with someone who sits around feeling sorry for him or herself. People are more willing to support you when you are ready to help your self.

Playing to win means taking charge of your life—to launch your self in a positive direction. It is living according to a high standard—valuing all that you are and living with wisdom. Playing to win means maintaining a bright attitude and outlook and developing your gifts and abilities—whatever they may be. It is making wholesome choices and answering for the choices you make.

The clutch player, the team and the crowd share the thrill of a game-winning jump shot. In this same way, playing to win is conducting your life in a manner that enriches both you and the human community.

The Hook Up

Nothing in life is really separate or disconnected from something else. Everything is related. We all have a responsibility to ourselves and to the human community. It is as though everyone is part of one great team working together, whether we are aware of this connection or not. We are hooked up at a subconscious level to work with and through one another to learn and grow. And like a team, what you do affects the whole in some positive or negative way. Think about that. Think about how everything you do from the moment you wake up in the morning to the time you go to bed at night affects others. It could be as simple as saying hello to acknowledge a stranger. That acknowledgement could make someone's day. It could be spreading malicious gossip, which could damage someone's self-esteem or reputation. It could be volunteering to tutor a child whose own parents are illiterate, and by doing this you give that child hope and promise. Or it could be cutting class and doing drugs which can ultimately corrupt your life and break your parents' hearts. It could be saying "no" to peer pressure, and instead, studying diligently for a science test and acing that test. You pass the course with flying colors, which prepares you for higher training. Ultimately, you may become a chemist who discovers a cure for a major disease. And that certainly impacts the lives of many others.

Because everything you do affects others, it makes you responsible for your thoughts and actions. And because you are responsible for your actions you must always try to make sure that you apply yourself in the most positive and productive way. This does not mean that you have to monitor your behavior all the time. It means thinking and acting in the best interests of your self and others. When you do this you will naturally behave responsibly.

What's Your Story?

Before you know where you are going you must know where you are coming from. You have decisions to make on how you are going to navigate and meet the world and respond to pressure and challenges. But you must first decide if you are going to participate and make the effort—to play to win or wander around in the parking lot. This is an important decision, which begins with where you are right now. So what's your story?

Inner City Teen

You live in a neighborhood that seems to be isolated and separate from society. It seems to have its own laws and codes of behavior. It is hard and scary outside, and you do not feel safe or free to find and be your self. Your family struggles with just about everything: Money, emotions, health and their ability to give you support and hope for your future. You may even be abused in a dysfunctional family, which is preoccupied with survival. And school just ain't happening. It's a joke, a waste of time. You feel some hurt, anguish and anxiety about many things. The options you see before you are limited and few. It would be easy to have a baby to fill the emptiness in your life; to join a gang in order to fit in, or to simply fade-out. You might even expect to die young.

Displaced and Homeless Teen

You had been living with your grandmother because your mother and father are not able to care and provide for you. Your grandmother struggles with money and resources and is being evicted from her home. She can no longer shelter you. Now you are on your own, but too young to take care of your self. Your options are to live with adult friends or go into a youth shelter. You are bright but it is hard to be motivated and focused with the distractions of not having a stable home and support.

OR. Home life is 'messed up'. Parents don't want to live right or are on your back 24/7 for just about everything. They don't understand you and you don't understand them. You can't have your way and are tired of the drama. Everything there is going negative. You want to be free. So you leave.

Peer-Pressured Teen

You are ridiculed on a daily basis, by schoolmates, who tease you about your weight and good grades. They 'signify' and 'dump' on you. They try to make people dislike you. You are a sensitive and naturally shy person who has a hard time facing this harassment and rejection each day. So you spend many of your lunch periods sitting in the corner of the library where the teasers can't find you. You know that if you stop studying and hang with them, you'll be safe. Your parents are there for you, but their love and support does not take away the pain of rejection. You want so much to fit in and be liked as you are. You think that if they only knew what a loving friend you can be they would treat you differently. Your depression about all this drives you to eat more and cry more, and your school performance is beginning to slide due to your low self-esteem.

OR. You are the teen who goes along with the group. If you don't, you know that they won't like you and will reject you. And you can't handle that. In order for you to be accepted by the group you hide a part of your self, because if you are your true self, they will tease and make fun of you. So you become what they want you to be, act the way they want you to act; you go along with what they do—even at times when you know that it is wrong. You don't want to rock the boat. And when you work so hard to impress and hang with them, you know that they still don't respect you, and that they will 'drop' you in a minute it suits them.

The "Big Bad Bully" Teen

You are scared of people who are not afraid of you, and you gravitate to them. But you prey on those you see as weak and vulnerable. You take advantage of *them* because you know you can get away with it. You tease them, you belittle them; you play pranks on them or you muscle things away from them; you may even hurt them with your hands. You like to do these things with an audience or crew watching so that they can see how strong or 'bad' you are. You feed on the suffering you bring to others and the negative attention it brings. And you like it when people are afraid of you. But deep down inside you are afraid. You don't know how to love your self, and you are fearful that people will find this out. You bully others to hide this secret.

The "Chip-on-the-Shoulder" Teen

You've got attitude for days! Been angry for so long you forgot what you are mad about. In fact, you don't even know that you are! It's part of your "front". It's what people expect, its what you put out. Anger comes natural to you. You attract attention to your self by showing off, trying to impress with your sarcasm—saving face and serving EGO, at all costs. No one gets to you and nobody leaves having the last word on you either. You are always right, and people either owe you something or they're out to get you. It's the teachers' fault that you are failing in school. It's your parents' fault that you fight at home; because they talk too much about what you should and should not do. You feel that it's too bad that people can't get with your program, and that you have to keep on putting up with their stupidity.

Privileged and Jaded Teen

You live in a prestigious, wealthy and protected community. You want for little or nothing. You go to a well-financed school where you are surrounded by people who look and act like you. The stage is set that guarantees your access to success because of your parents' connections and position in society. Yet despite this, you are depressed, anxious and doing drugs. You have gone from experimenting with marijuana to regular use of harder drugs which you do while cutting class. Like the drugs, you are finding the cynicism that your 'friends' have for any and everything comforting and cool.

"Down With Whatever" Teen

Your wardrobe is tight with the latest fly styles. And your arsenal of hard core and 'gangsta' rap is stacked. You are learned in the word, moves and slang. You hang out *only* with your 'homies'. They are your family because you know they've got your back. Ain't nothing wrong with hip hop, but you like to 'get low'. Your mind is on how to keep up with what's going down, which changes fast. But you don't miss a beat. You may even be a player moving in on a hook-up with a bitch or a 'ho'. No problem. It all comes so easy and maybe you subscribe to the role put to you by a loose code of conduct—placing little value on your self as a young woman. Your body is a main attraction and you get a lot of play. That's 'dough', because you are 'down with whatever'.

The Teen Who Isn't There

You don't seem to make an impression on people. Not the kids at school or your family. When you talk, no one really listens. When you show up, no one notices. It seems that people don't go out of their way to get to know you. You don't have many friends. And this bothers you. Your parents are busy with their affairs: Work, TV or their own life and friends. They give you everything but themselves. You occupy a space in your house and a desk at school. But you really aren't there. Inside you are screaming to be seen and heard. You really want to connect. The fact that you can't is beginning to make you angry and resentful.

All Dressed Up and No 'Way' To Go Teen

You may seem to have it all together. You may have supportive parents, good schooling, grades and friends. You have a level head and a sense of where you want to go. You are self-possessed and are guided by what is right and appropriate. But what you are beginning to experience is that you have certain questions that are not being answered. You have issues and problems that are not easily solved or understood. Life is complex and things are happening too fast. You have to make choices and decisions that are difficult for you. Although you are willing and ready to give it your best shot, the road ahead is blurry and intimidating.

ᕙᔕ ᕙᔕ ᕙᔕ

You may find your story among one of these, or you may find pieces of your story in a few or all of them. You are most likely one of many teens who are facing a dynamic world with inadequate tools to make your way despite your race, culture or social class. Many young people like you see life through these windows. They experience some the same things you experience, such as confusion, anger, resentment, apathy, low self-esteem and self- doubt. They become discouraged, laissez-faire and careless with their lives. They lose their self-respect and compromise their youth. The light that is always within them does not shine. And for many, the ultimate way out is suicide. This is not the way it is supposed to be.

Your choice to 'work' the game and play to win moves you beyond the limitations of any of these scenarios. It is the *first step* you take on your journey to become a winning adult.

Teens At Risk

There are circumstances you were born into that impact how you will move through life. You are only 'at-risk' when you do not step around them, and when they overcome and hold you down. A teen of any race, culture, ethnicity, class or background can be 'at risk'. The circumstances that place teens 'at risk' fall into three categories:

At Risk Category One

These teens have been subjected to a crisis situation. They are runaways, throwaways, abused, drop-outs—or have had some tragic experience that impaired their emotional health. They are products of broken homes, or from a high-risk dysfunctional family situation in which they were negatively impacted. As a result of these experiences these teens have become mentally unfocused, emotionally unstable or scarred. They have anger and resentment. They have no interest in goals and they typically have a chip on their shoulder.

At Risk Category Two

These teens are in school and have acquired some training to get jobs. But they lack other necessary skills in order to be successful in those jobs. They do not have the people skills, communication skills, political or social skills that employers look for, and that are required to function in today's society. And they have limited resources available to help them develop these skills. These teens are not able to interface with work teams, the larger society or diverse groups of people. They have a limited scope and view of life. A common example is of the high school student who objected to the presence of *white* visitors at her school. When they came to her classroom she complained angrily: "What the *bleep* are they doing here!" She saw the *white* visitors as intruders in the all *black* high school. She refused to meet and talk with these visitors who were there to offer free corporate internships to students at her school. This kind of 'at-risk' behavior prevents these teens from expanding their world, embracing opportunities, and it keeps them in a box.

At Risk Category Three

These teens do not come from crises situations and they may have the proper skills required to succeed. But they are 'at-risk' because they do not have fair access to opportunities to apply their skills. This is due to institutional racism and bias in social systems that are set up to block them.

⁂ ⁂ ⁂

Whether you are 'at risk' or not, your young life may seem to be over or decided before it has begun. You may believe you are limited by circumstances or restricted to play a role already defined by those around you. You may feel anxious, fearful, doubtful, or even angry about these things. Or because much has been given to you so early in life and so easily, nothing seems new to you—you may not see possibilities or openings. Instead, you have become bored, spoiled or rebellious. Perhaps you are blinded by too many distractions, illusions and *bling*; and you have become unfocused, jaded or disinterested. Maybe you just don't like what you see going on in the world. Nothing hooks you in. I know you often feel alone with your problems—as if few or no one understands or can connect with you. I know the hopelessness you may feel. I know the fear. And I know the rage. I know you may feel that you have been let down. But I ask you—despite your scenario, who is going to live for you?

Your young, precious life needs to be lived. "At risk" circumstances are there for you to overcome. So you have work to do. Like the gifted point guard, you must step up to the ball coming at you, and with swift precision, poise and resolve, grab and slam-dunk it!

Take another step forward!

In the Spirit!

Meet spirit! Spirit is the primary life force. It is pure, positive, creative power. Spirit is life giving and life supporting. Everything you do is connected to spirit. Spirit power works with the energy of your thoughts, beliefs and feelings to create your experiences. It does this in the same way your breath fills your lungs and fuels your body. The union of your mental/emotional energies and spiritual forces forms your *'higher power'*. This is what makes you *a spiritual being.*

What is Spiritual Law?

There are numerous natural laws that govern diverse aspects of our lives. There are laws of mathematics, physics, biology, nature and so on. Even though these laws may not be easy to understand, they are constant, perfect, and absolute. They are at the foundation of what makes life what it is, from the sunrise to an airplane's flight; from a mathematical riddle, to the miracle of the internet. We know these laws exist. We simply relax into their authority and certainty, and let them do their thing.

Spiritual laws are among these natural laws. Life is essentially a creative process, and spiritual laws govern how your thoughts, feelings and beliefs manifest into reality. *For example,* the laws of physics that make a computer or cell phone work, or that lifts an airplane into the air and keeps it in flight operate in the realm of science and technology; while the laws that help you create your life through your thoughts, feelings and beliefs operate in the realm of spirit.

When you do the math it looks like this:

In the Spirit

Spirit + your thoughts, beliefs and feelings = your experiences and reality

How Does Spiritual Law Affect You?

This is the 'real deal' and the bottom line. If you can think it, believe it and expect it, you can be it. You have many resources available to you to make your way successfully in the world. They include education, community development and enrichment programs, parents, teachers, counselors, mentor programs, internships, libraries, good health, supportive friends, and much more. Of all the resources you have, however, the greatest is within you.

According to spiritual law, the most awesome power you have at your command is your power to control what you believe, think, feel and do. This is called *free will* or *choice*. This puts you in charge of your life, either positively or negatively. Just as you drive a car by turning the wheel, you steer your life in any direction you want through your free will and choices. If you know what you want, and truly believe that you deserve it, and if you apply your self to achieve what you desire, then you will have the thing that you want. If you don't know what you want, then life will give you just anything. And just anything may not be what you want. In either case, your free will and choices are still driving the car, whether into a dead end or onto the open highway!

Powerful spiritual laws become your allies as you create the life and experiences you want. These laws are perfect and they are sovereign. They are already working in your life whether you are aware of them or not. Your goal is to engage this positive spiritual force and direct it to work to your advantage. And you do this by maintaining positive thoughts, beliefs and taking positive directions.

Your openness and willingness to work with spiritual law brings its mighty arms to you—wrapping around your life. In this embrace you experience positivity, well-being, abundance and success. In the same way that a fetus receives nourishment from its mother's body through the umbilical cord, your life is nourished through your mind's connection with spirit. The hands of spirit help you to shape your life the way you want. All things become possible. In essence, spiritual laws bring you those experiences that match your thoughts, beliefs and feelings. What you think and feel strongly about you begin to believe. And what you truly believe and expect you eventually bring into reality. The creative forces will always respond with a 'yes' to your deepest desires and expectations. Whether those desires or expectations are positive or negative, they will be met!

The diagram on the following page illustrates the relationship between spiritual and other natural laws.

Before you are black, white, male, female, rich or poor, you are a spiritual being! And as a spiritual being you are innately bound by spiritual law, which flows in your life just as blood flows through your veins.

The more you learn about your mind, emotions and spiritual nature, the more you will understand how these laws work, and the more you will flow with them.

To work positively and in harmony with spiritual laws you must:

1. Accept that you are responsible for what you create through your thoughts, beliefs, feelings and choices.

2. Through your free will choose right-thought and right-action.

3. Commit to applying your self, do the work—understand and 'work' the connection between mind and spirit.

4. Listen to and follow the voice of spirit.

Many of your champions would tell you that by doing these things they became famous, accomplished and successful. They knew what they wanted and took responsibility to create it. They acted in the best interests of themselves and others. They sacrificed and did the work. And they respected and aligned with a Higher Spiritual Power. You have this same potential. And you have it because it comes with being human and having a basic spiritual nature.

Keep on steppin'!

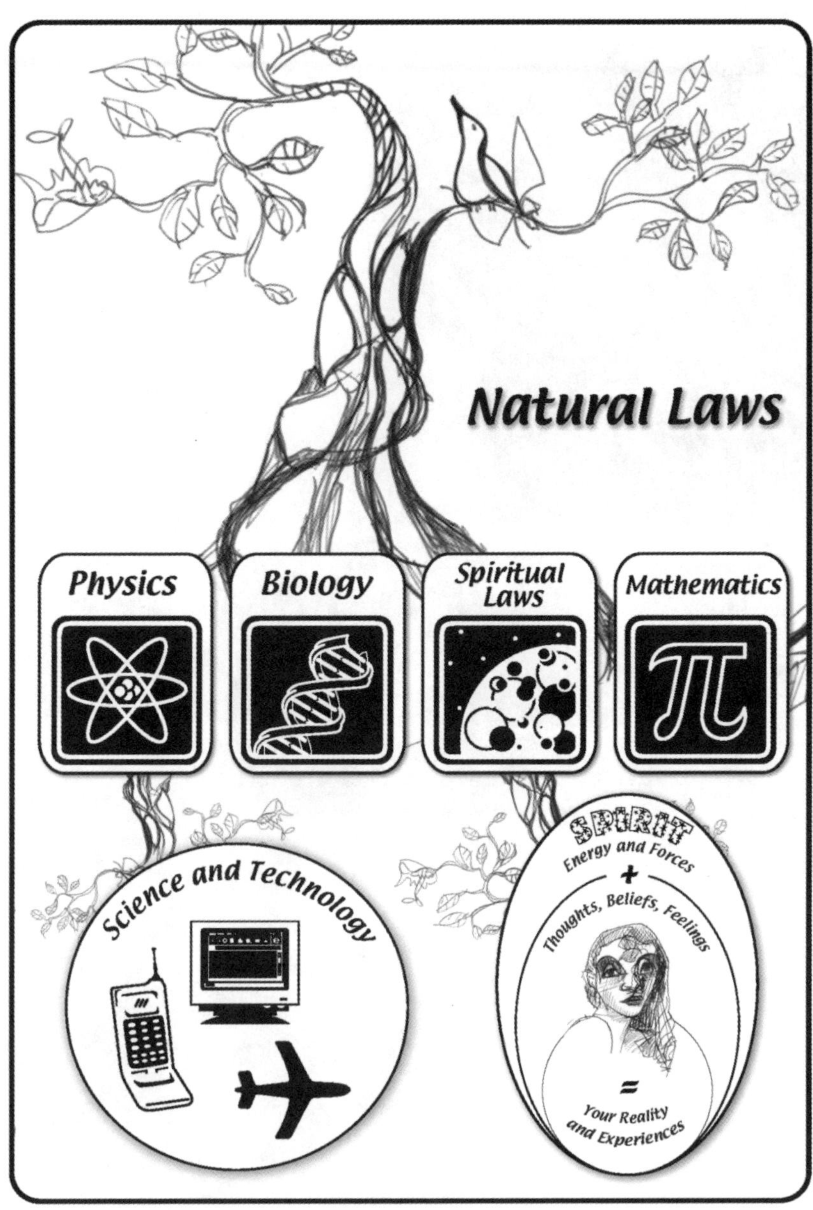

In the Spirit

Chapter Two

You Got Game!

To whom much is given, much is required.
—Tavis Smiley

*By childhood a person should have selected
the purpose of his or her life.*
—Muhammad Ali

*Lift up your eyes upon this day breaking for you.
Give birth again to the dream.*
—Maya Angelou

The Joy of Self-Discovery

You were born perfect and unique! Things may have happened in your life along the way to becoming a teen to make you lose track of this fact. Perhaps what you came here to actualize got warped or misplaced by upbringing or conditioning. But that can be changed and straightened out. You can choose to discover and define your self now—despite your past. You can choose to go back to square one and make known, the truth about you. When you look inside your self, free of history, you will be amazed with what you will find. You may strike gold that can catapult you to fabulous places. When you dig deep, you will find your gift and your purpose.

Everyone has a gift and purpose. It is a matter of personal choice whether or not a person identifies their gift and moves with their purpose. You come into this world already endowed with gifts. Your process of self-discovery will help you unveil these gifts and begin to put them to use.

Now that you've got 'word' and the 'hook-up', your most immediate goal is to discover the spark within, that you did not know existed. It may even be something that your parents did not recognize. Being a teen is a time of self-discovery. And you can have fun with this.

Self-discovery begins with stopping the noise and activity around you and in your daily affairs. It is taking a 'time out' to observe your life and do some personal inventory. There are some questions you need to ask your self. So go to your room or your private space, get quiet with your self, and plan to spend some good time exploring these questions:

1. What is the most outstanding thing I am experiencing now?

2. What kinds of people are in my life and that I surround myself with?

3. How do people respond to me and treat me? What do they say about me?

4. What am I doing most of the time?

5. What do I do well and enjoy doing?

6. What do I gravitate to most?

7. What gives me joy?

8. What do I think about and feel most?

9. What am I noticed and rewarded for most often?

10. What gets my attention, gets me excited and makes me dream?

Asking your self these kinds of questions will lead you to your gift and purpose. Keep exploring these questions until your gift and purpose become clear. You will continue to discover things about your self. It is a long and winding road that will change and veer right and left throughout your life. But it must begin now! Keep a journal and make this discovery process a part of your routine.

This is also an exercise that you can do with a parent, counselor or coach. But make sure that YOU spend most of the time thinking about these things. It is important that you OWN this process.

Your Gift and Purpose

Your gift is a natural ability that you possess. Your gift becomes your talent when it is something that you do very well and that you enjoy doing. Your gift becomes a talent when it can be put into the world as a vocation, a service, or both. You will encounter many opportunities to turn your gifts into talents.

You are happier and life is more fulfilling when you build a career around your gifts and talents. This insures that the career you pursue will also have a future.

How do you know when you have found your gift? Your gift is the one thing inside you that won't let you go. It talks to you late at night and wakes you up early in the morning. It is something inside that you've got to make happen. You know it is your gift because 'you just do it'. It is called a 'gift' because it is given to you for you to give to others. When you 'lock in' to your gift you can affect and infect people. *Star Shine Academy** is an organization that helps young people find their unique talents, and supports those talents with inspiration and encouragement; and by integrating mind, body and spirit.

Your purpose is what you are here to achieve by using your gift. And you have unlimited options. You may be a gifted artist and become an entertainer. You may be a gifted writer who will produce many books. You may be gifted with a loving and nurturing nature, which will lead you into caretaking roles for people in need. You may have a good mind for numbers and analyzing and may become a scientist or educator. You may be gifted at organizing information and research and may start your own business. Or you may have a natural sense of fairness and may become a social justice lawyer and then a judge. Any gift can be honed into a talent to put into the world.

Your Role in the Greater Scheme of Things

You are here for a reason. Your life has value, purpose and meaning! You are part of the human community, and your talent and contribution are essential to the betterment of all. The world is full of problems, crises and conflicts that need to be resolved. There is much joy to be harvested, spirit to be raised, and triumph to be engineered. People from both humble and noble beginnings have made a difference in the world. And because you have a vital role to play, there is nothing good nor bad, nor shameful or inferior about you, despite your circumstances, status in life, race or cultural background. Period!

Spirit's plan is that you apply your gifts towards creating a life that is joyful for you. Spirit's plan is that your gifts make the world a better place, and brings about a positive change in other peoples' lives. Most vocations and callings in life are avenues for you to do this.

You are part of a divine plan and are here to make a contribution. You are an agent of spirit's design. When your purpose aligns with spirit's plan you are its instrument, its partner, its cherished soul.

Being An Original

Once you have connected with your unique gift, you must respect and to step with it into the world. Don't be afraid to be different. You should not be led by the flavor of the month. Many teens believe that they must be 'down' with the latest trend. But many trends today are someone else's dream. Its better to be your own 'trend influence'. You want to be an original, not an impersonator, copycat or imposter. You go much farther in life by being genuine—your true self. And being an original is easier to do than you think! Its fun, it makes you more interesting and enables you to get more out of life.

Cases in point: Shani Davis, an African-American, inner city youth was ridiculed by his peers because he was 'different' and choose to pursue speed skating. He focused and developed his talent and went on to win an Olympic Gold medal in 2006; and Norah Jones, a biracial woman, who committed to honing her unique and pure talent for music during her teens. She took some risks that lead her to produce a phenomenal album that swept the Grammys in 2003.

Before locking into any style or 'mode of operating', ask your self, *"Does this feel right and natural to me?"* And *"Who am I doing this for?"* If your answers are: *"Yes"* and *"I'm feeling that"*—then lock in. You own it.

You've Got This!

When the game of life has you mystified, duped, hoodwinked and bamboozled, you can still shake it off and roll. Your turn is still coming up. As they say, "It ain't nuthin' but a party!"

You are stepping into a chapter full of wonder and promise. On the one hand, you have openings and possibilities as never before. You can access your boldest dreams. You can pursue any vocation you want, because you were born perfect and have something to offer. There are resources and support out there that match your drive, ambition and talent. On the other hand you make hard choices now. There are hurdles you must overcome that far differ from those your parents faced as teens. Traditional ways of living and 'making it' are giving way to newer, 'out-of-the-box' lifestyles.

You've got this! With spirit as your ally and your arsenal of *positive attitude, vision, skills, commitment, wisdom and free will to make responsible choices*, you can rise to any occasion. You will have the resolve to resist negative peer pressure. You will make sensible choices around sex, drugs, gangbanging and other non-productive behaviors. You will craft a vision and cultivate skills to carry it. You will commit! With this formula in the mix you will make your way into the world, give your gift, and your personal best, and live the life you want. The more you do this, the better you will get at it; and the more you will shift your life from pain and fear and into joy.

So light it up! And give it up!

*Star Shine Academy. Starshineacademy.org.

Chapter Three

Family and Relationships

*I had not father or mother; I am alone in the world. If I had
a father or a mother like you, I would be with them and
they with me.*
                    —Cochise of the Chiricahua Apaches

*The family you come from isn't as important as the family
you're going to have.*
                    —Ring Lardner

Your primary support as a teen and as an adult will come from family and relationships. A relationship is a connection to someone through blood, values, interests, history or experience. A family is a relationship. You may consider your close friends as family. But it all boils down to getting along with other people. And you do this with your mother, father, siblings, friends, teachers, counselors, work associates, neighbors, and so on. Good relationships require effort and should not be taken for granted. As a teen it is time to uphold the relationships in your life, to take them seriously, and do your part to nurture and sustain them. Supportive relationships are the foundation of a well-lived life.

A Family Is as a Family Does

Your biological family is your first relationship. You were born into it. In fact, this is the one relationship that you do not hand pick, it happens to you. But there are many kinds of families. Your parents can be your biological mother and father, a relative or friend who acts as your guardian. A family can be the caretakers and other youths in a group home or shelter. Your family can be the people who share your household, and who may or may not share your ancestry. There is no special recipe for what makes a 'happy' family. Although it can be ideal, it is not always advantageous to live with both mother and father. Many of the world's brightest stars came from single-parent homes or were adopted. And the worst public offenders grew up with both their natural mothers and fathers in the home. What matters is the core of love and support you get from your family unit, no matter who the people who make up that unit may be. And as you move out into the world, your family will expand and include your closest friends, teachers and mentors.

Helping Your Family to Help You

You are fortunate if you have one or two loving, caring parents who are there for you when you need them. But even then, they cannot and should not do all the work for you in order for you to grow well. Different parents have their own ways of showing support and caring for their children. When they do this, work with them. Help them to help you. Help is help, regardless of their generation, values or style. And you need all the assistance you can get now. You may not understand them or why they use the tactics they do. But try to appreciate the fact that they are there to benefit you. And to a great extent, you need them. Trust them. Open up to them. Talk to them. Let them know what is going on. Tell them your stories, your needs and where you want to go in life.

Give these parents support as best you can because they too, are still growing and have a lot to learn from you. Your parents are dealing with many pressures, which may include finances, work demands, or their own family issues. They are also challenged to learn and grow, like you. In fact, they experience more pressure than you. Try to learn from your parents' experiences. Try to understand their stresses, struggles and responsibilities, because these may someday be your own. You can always find ways to make your parents' lives easier. When you do this, you are also making your home life with parents more relaxed. Because when they can deal with their pressures they are better able to respond to your needs.

When Your Family Cannot Help You

There are some parents who mean well, but do not have the ability or the skills to nurture and support their children's growth needs. These parents can barely take care of themselves. There are also parents who are basically, still children, and have not matured emotionally or psychologically. They are unable to handle life's pressures and responsibilities. They may even become self-destructive and abusive. Many teens have these kinds of parents. Parents or other relatives betray your trust by not responding to your needs for love, appreciation, recognition and respect. The way you were affected as a child due to parents' behavior, however, does not have to control you all your life. It does not have to cripple or destroy you. Parents who were not there for you psychologically, emotionally or physically were caught up in their own fears and insecurities.

When your family cannot or will not be there for you, it makes you grow up fast. You seek substitutes to fill that empty space. You try to find ways to take care of your needs. You may try to feed your self, fend for your self, build your self up, or gravitate to someone else to take care of you. Understand that these pressures to take custody of your self or to go without essential parental care are unnatural, and this is not your fault. Do not, for a minute, think that there is something wrong with you, or that you do not deserve these things. There is a reason for everything that happens to you. And there must be something very special about you that caused life to deal you these cards. Know that even in this situation you are making choices about what you think, feel and believe. Hold on! And do the right thing. With each day that you are alive and growing, things are getting better.

Divorce

Today, almost half of marriages end in divorce. Divorce is a hard reality that many teens face. Teens handle divorce differently. Some take it in stride while others struggle and find it difficult to accept. In either case, divorce marks a major change in your life that will impact you. It changes your relationship with mother and father. However, it does not necessarily mean that those relationships are gone. Whether you live with two parents or with one, what matters is the continuity of support, nurture, guidance, and positive role modeling you receive. Divorce should not diminish your needs. And you can and should let both parents remember and know what is important to you.

I have yet to hear about a divorce that was caused by the children. So understand that *the divorce* is not your fault, and you are not to blame, nor are you the one to try to put things back together. That is a burden that you don't need. In fact, it is unrealistic. Try not to resent your parents for making the decision to separate. Grant them the freedom to learn and grow from this choice. In many cases divorce releases tensions in the family unit and makes room for new energy to come in. It frees family members from pain and anguish and revitalizes family relationships, often taking them into more rewarding directions. If you cannot let go of the fact that mom and dad are no longer together, tell them so, and ask them to help you deal with it. Don't keep the hurt in and allow it to fester. If they cannot help you or respond, share your feelings with another responsible adult or family member. Your goal here is to stay focused and make certain that your attitudes and behavior are shaped by your strengths, not your weaknesses, and that you do not stay stuck in the past.

Sarah's Story

Sarah is a 19 year-old Jewish teen. Her parents had a bitter divorce when she was 16. Sarah's father is quite wealthy. However, the divorce left her mother in extreme financial hardship. Sarah lives with her father and her younger sister lives with her mother. The relationship between Sarah's parents is hostile and toxic. Sarah has much anger towards her mother, whom her father describes as mentally disturbed, unstable and a bad person. Sarah refuses to see or have anything to do with her mother. Sarah is also beginning to experience much conflict in her relations with other people in her life. She is unmotivated, has no goals and hangs around the house while relying on her father for financial support.

My observation here is that Sarah is not separating her father's pain and anger towards her mother from her own feelings, which might be very different. She is under the spell of her parents' divorce. Sarah is also buying in to her father's anger in order to win his support, both emotional and financial. But the price she is paying is very high. She is depleted by the continued conflict between her parents to the point that she can do nothing positive with her own life. Sarah needs to understand that both her parents are in pain and that their behavior, even her father's, is dictated by this pain. She needs to get real and stop fooling herself by making her parents' problems an excuse to do nothing with her life. She needs to give her mother the benefit of the doubt, which will help to bring her own emotions into balance. And Sarah needs to look at the anger that she is carrying and see how it is infecting her life, then make some important choices.

Teen Homelessness

There is a growing epidemic of homeless teens. Not all teens today live with their natural families or in a surrogate family unit. These teens, ranging from ages 13 through 19 become homeless, largely due to physical, emotional or sexual abuse at home. They either leave these situations or are cast out. Some become homeless when they reach legal age and are released from juvenile centers, or youth homes. Other teens voluntarily exit a home life that they feel is intolerable and where they cannot have their way. While many are displaced when their parents' states-of-mind or lifestyles are unstable, and they have no other family unit in which to go. And there are those teens that are simply abandoned. The army of homeless teens is increasing at an alarming rate.

Many teens on the streets have acquiesced to this way of life. They are called '*millrats*', while other teens desperately want some kind of rescue. Homeless teens form a loose family unit made up of other street teens and/or the staff from youth agencies that reach out to them. *Home Base** is one such agency. Located in Phoenix, Arizona, *Home Base* teaches 'at-risk' and homeless teens to live healthy and independently. They take youth off the streets and place them into caring shelters. On a daily basis, *Home Base* teams go out to teens living in parks or desolate parts of the city, and provide them with food, toiletries, socks or medical supplies. They make job training, GED preparation, advice and love available to all homeless teens—those living within the shelter or on the outside.

If you are living on the streets or at the risk of becoming homeless, learn about the support agencies that are there for you. As teen homelessness increases, so do these services! It's not fun out there. Although hanging out may appear freeing and intriguing at the beginning, it gets tired and stagnates you. You can't get ahead on the streets. Life passes you by as you indulge in idleness. And if you are in a situation at home that can lead to you being 'thrown out', try to use the tools provided in this book about communication and relationships. For these are the key reasons why things don't go well at home. Above all, do all you can to stay in from the cold.

Hector's Story

Hector is a 16 year-old Hispanic teen at risk of becoming displaced from his home. He is not happy and is habitually looking for ways to stay out of the house. He complains that his mother nags and never really listens to him. He says that his mother always takes his stepfather's side, and that his stepfather does not like him and is too hard on him. Hector has been thrown out of three high schools within a 2-year period for 'tagging' school property. And these ejections occurred after he was repeatedly warned to stop. When I asked Hector why he continued to tag despite these outcomes, he replied that he is a good artist and that I should see his stuff. He wants people to notice his work and tagging is the only way to do this. Hector gets into fights easily because he is physically aggressive and short tempered. He also gets into trouble from playing telephone pranks. Hector has a lot of nervous energy and talks excessively. One can hardly get a word in with him.

My observation here is that Hector does the same thing that he accuses his mother of doing—not listening. Initially, I would like to see Hector acknowledge and take responsibility for his behavior, to listen more, and to find constructive ways to express his talent for art, and to spend his energy. I would like to see him find a responsible male mentor within his family or community to discuss his family concerns. From my last contact with Hector, I learned that he had moved in with an uncle and is about to attend military school.

Relationships

There is very little you can do or achieve in life that does not involve people. Your primary family relationships have gotten you this far. Now you are expanding beyond the safety net of a family circle and beginning to surround your self with other people. These relationships will matter a great deal. These are relationships that will be both assigned to you and that you will select. These are the relationships that will make or break you. They are with teachers, counselors, work associates, friends, neighbors, classmates, etc. These relationships will impact you emotionally, mentally, financially, and physically. They will bring you pain and they will bring you joy.

It is time for you to pay more attention to the many people who come into your life, and to pay more attention to how you show up with them. You need these relationships, because through them, you learn and grow. They amplify your life. The key here is to understand that you are now able and required to make healthy choices about *who* participates in your circle of life and *how.*

Understand that the manner in which you relate to someone determines how that person will treat you. You choose your friends, and you choose how you are going to conduct those relations that were assigned to you—with teachers, work associates, counselors, neighbors, etc. Strive to do this responsibly and with your right mind. And choose to connect in a positive and civil manner with the people you meet causally. This includes store clerks, service people, bank tellers, school administrators and so on. The ability to meet, greet and treat people well will enhance your life, enormously.

Keep in mind that many people today are experiencing tremendous stress and anxiety. Plus, the social index of fear and anger is high. Stress, anxiety, fear and anger combined with poor interpersonal skills can be lethal—keeping people on a short fuse. Be very discerning about who enters your life. You don't have to accept anyone. Choose people who are emotionally responsible and stable.

What You Can Do

1. *Get to know your self.* Make this a priority! Whether home life is hoppin' or gives you the blues; it may be time to take care of your business. This begins by asking your self some questions: *"Who am I? What do I like? What don't I like? How do I feel most of the time? What makes me happy? Sad? How do I show up, and is that working? Am I a shy or outgoing person? What are my strengths and weaknesses? How do my strengths help me, and how do my weaknesses trip me up?"* These are the kinds of questions that lead to self-knowledge, understanding and eventually, self-mastery. By asking these questions whether you come up with the answers or not, you learn to think more for your self and establish your independence. And self-knowledge enables you to better respond to the challenges that come your way.

A supportive family should always be a resource for guidance and nurturing. But you are growing now and part of this growth is to take a good look at YOU and how you function. Sometimes deep problems and challenges in the family are signs that it is time to do this—to learn where family problems end and your life begins.

Self-knowledge spans a lifetime. People are always changing and growing out of their old selves and into new ones. But there is something you can do as a rule to keep sight of who you are. Become intimately acquainted with what you think about most, what you believe about your self, and what you expect from your self. All you have to do is stop and listen to your mind, spirit and heart.

2. *Write your own script.* Make it a habit to see your self in a positive light. Remember, abusive parents' attitudes and behaviors towards you do not tell the truth about who you are. Their attitudes have more to do with their problems. The truth about you is that you are responsible for your self and how you are going to think, behave and respond to situations. Learn to reject negative opinions about you that come from abusive people and create your own positive ones. Simply re-write the script to read: *"What that person thinks and says about me is not true. I am worthwhile, attractive, talented, and I am going places!"*

3. ***Don't make your parents' problems your problems.*** Behind your parents' worried frowns there may be heavy burdens, stress, finances, conflict with others or conflict within themselves. Anything! But don't take these on. They don't belong to you. Don't make your parents' shortcomings an excuse for you to fail or let your self down. *For example:* Avoid feeling that you don't have to be responsible for your self because your parents aren't around, or because they may have irresponsible habits or lifestyles. Avoid saying to

your self *"I don't have to go to school today because my dad stayed out all night,"* or *"I don't have to make good grades because my mom doesn't pay attention to what I do anyway."*

The more you make your parents' problems your own, the more you will be bound and controlled by their problems. These troubles will consume your life and prevent you from growing. And when you don't grow, you only hurt your self.

4. ***Try to understand.*** Try putting your self into your parents' shoes to better understand their behavior and the choices they made. Try not to judge them as being right or wrong, but having made bad choices that hurt themselves and those around them, including you.

    Try to understand where your parents are coming from. But do not make excuses for them. Maybe they have limited opportunities, weak personalities, or legitimate handicaps that hold them back. Maybe something happened in their life that broke them down—something they never recovered from. Maybe you are in a better position to help them than they are to help you. If you realize this and can assist your parents, do so in a way that does not hold you back. Remember that helping someone is very different than taking care of them. And don't give in to any abuse; remain loyal to your self.

5. ***Nurture your parents.*** Parents need to be nurtured also. They, like you, need to be energized with love, affection and attention. And there are healthy ways for you to do this. For one, be aware that all human relations are energy exchanges. Positive relations energize and bless, while negative relations de-energize, depress and even cause conflict. Take this into your understanding as you communicate with your parents. Nurture parents with compliments and support and concern for their challenges and responsibilities.

Tone down the petty grief and disagreements that drain you both. Strive for positive energy exchanges with them.

Also don't always expect parents to initiate conversation or interactions with you. You can and should engage your parents. Show them that you are interested in their thing, and enjoy relating to them. This is not going to kill you! OK?

6. *Appreciate your parents' world, and their word.* The generation gap between parents and teens is normal. It is supposed to be there. It allows for the wisdom and experience from one generation to flow to the next. If your parents come across as 'old school' or do not connect with your style and vibe, consider that healthy. Because where there are age gaps there are openings for learning and bonding. And often, the larger the gap, the richer the growth opportunities for both parent and teen.

    Take the sweet with the bitter. As a rule, teens tend to feel persecuted by parents. They do this by only seeing the things that parents do to inconvenience, restrict or upset them, instead of also seeing what parents do that is beneficial, supportive and loving. Taking on this perception is a 'choice'. Know that it is also hard for parents to guide and teach you in ways that might make you bitter. When they don't do this, they are neglecting you. Trust your parents enough to see the good that they are doing which can outweigh the hard stuff, and appreciate how this is helping you along.

7. *Let your parents make mistakes.* Let them be human. Don't hold them to an unrealistic standard. As they make mistakes or fall short of your expectations, be patient with them and understand that they are still learning and growing. Try to learn from your parents' mistakes. It will save you grief in the long run.

And, avoid making assumptions about anything concerning your parents before checking it out with them. Ask them questions to clarify things, and be respectful when doing so. Give them the benefit of a doubt. It will bring you closer to them.

8. ***Let go.*** Resentment is like taking a poison and expecting the other person to die. Try not to dwell too long on how wronged you were by an abusive parent or other kinship. You have more to lose than to gain by allowing pain to fester inside you. Acknowledge and name the hurt, then work your self away from it and its source. Don't rely on abusive people for nurture, support or apologies. Reduce your expectations of them. Expecting too much from abusive people takes away your power to move forward with your life. This weakens you and gives them control over you. Like a puppet on a string.

Learn from the abuse by being proactive. Recognize when there are negative people in your life. Let go of those who threaten your welfare and development, even if they are parents or family members. Wish them well and wish them growth. And when you walk away, leave the anger and resentment behind. You don't want that to slow you down.

Realize that some people have not learned the concepts of nurture and support. They have not mined the wisdom to love themselves or others. It is easier for them to be hurtful and self-destructive. These people have a lot of growing to do.

Letting go and moving on does not mean that you stop loving your parents and family. You should keep the love you feel for them in your heart. But loving someone does not mean allowing that person to harm you or hold you back. You can love from a distance. Always keep your devotion to others in proper perspective to your growth needs.

9. *Go where there is life.* When you find your self in a toxic and unstable family situation that is not changing for the better, you need to do something. This does not mean moving out of the house. Sometimes this is not practical. You may not be able to take care of your self.

    You are going to have to thrive in that situation and make the best of it, either until you can be on your own or a miracle intervenes. And you start by going where there is life!

    You need a diversion to keep you from becoming consumed by a dysfunctional family environment. You need to establish your independence. When you are active in progressive extracurricular activities, and maintain an enlightened attitude about your self, you become more self-sufficient, self-reliant and self-ruling—less impacted by a chaotic family life. When you go where there is life, you find that things begin to fall into place for you.

    So get a hobby. Join the YMCA or a recreational club or team. Work on a committee or with a community youth group. You can find out about these things from schools or civic centers. *Girls for a Change** is one such organization that empowers 'at-risk' girls to create social change. The activities you choose should be enjoyable and make you feel that you are achieving, and are a part of something worthwhile. This kind of involvement shields you from negativity and gives you exposure to a brighter side of life. Through these activities you also grow your spirit.

    In the meantime do not provoke conflicts within the household or give in to the dysfunction. Try to bring some of the positive energy you are experiencing into that situation.

10. *Create an extended family.* Reach for strength and support where you can. Seek out relationships with people who will nurture you and support your growth. Approach someone

you know and trust, and ask for help. Accept their help if it is offered to you. Make sure this is someone who feels good about you and is responsible and respectful of your needs. Surround your self with these people and create an extended family. They may be relatives, friends, counselors or school personnel who can give you emotional or financial support, advice and counseling. Parents are not the only ones who can love and support you.

11. ***Find and treasure your family's gifts to you.*** You were born into a particular family for a reason. All family members have something to teach and give you. You learn and gain from their experiences and examples. They give you tokens from family life for your journey. Look deep into this treasure chest and see what you are taking away with you as you grow. Cherish these gifts.

12. ***Be straight up!—Brave the truth.*** A chief frustration for parents is that they are frequently lied to by their teens. And yes, teens easily resort to lies because it seems easier than braving the truth. Teens fear that something will be taken away from them, or something will happen to shake their world if the truth is told. A lie is a waste of time. It holds you up, and it blocks you. The fact is, that lying produces short-term relief, but long-term problems and inconveniences.

A lie is complicated and it complicates things. It makes you work hard to maintain and conceal it. It only delays what is inevitable, because sooner or later it will come back to you, and you will have to own up to it. And when it does, matters could be worse. A habit of lying can bring you a lot of pain as you grow into adulthood. Remember you lie because you are afraid. And you are better than that. So brave the truth. Truth gets things done the right way and the first time. It clears you and lets you move on.

Q & A
Frequently Asked Questions by Teens

"Do parents need to know everything about me? "

<u>*Answer:*</u> Some kids create situations that require high parental scrutiny, while greater levels of trust between other parents and teens require less scrutiny. So it really depends on your behavioral record and your parent's style. Ultimately, parents cannot and will not know everything about you, but spiritual law has a way of eventually bringing things to the light.

"What if my parents tell me to do one thing and they turn around and do another, acting like hypocrites?

<u>*Answer*</u>: Even though parents may know right from wrong they may not always act accordingly. "Do as I say, not as I do" certainly applies here. There are many things that your parents can do that you cannot do that are within the domain of parenting. You must respect and honor this and also the fact that they are still growing. When you feel that your parent is being hypocritical, look beyond their actions and look at their intentions. You know deep down inside that your parents mean you well when they tell you to do one thing while they do another. Trust that they are trying to protect and guide you from becoming trapped in the patterns and behaviors they may display.

Also, what comes across as hypocritical behavior, may just be an example of how hard it is to change old, bad habits. Try to appreciate this and learn from it.

**Home Base Youth Services. www.hbys.org*
**Girls for a Change. www.girlsforachange.com*

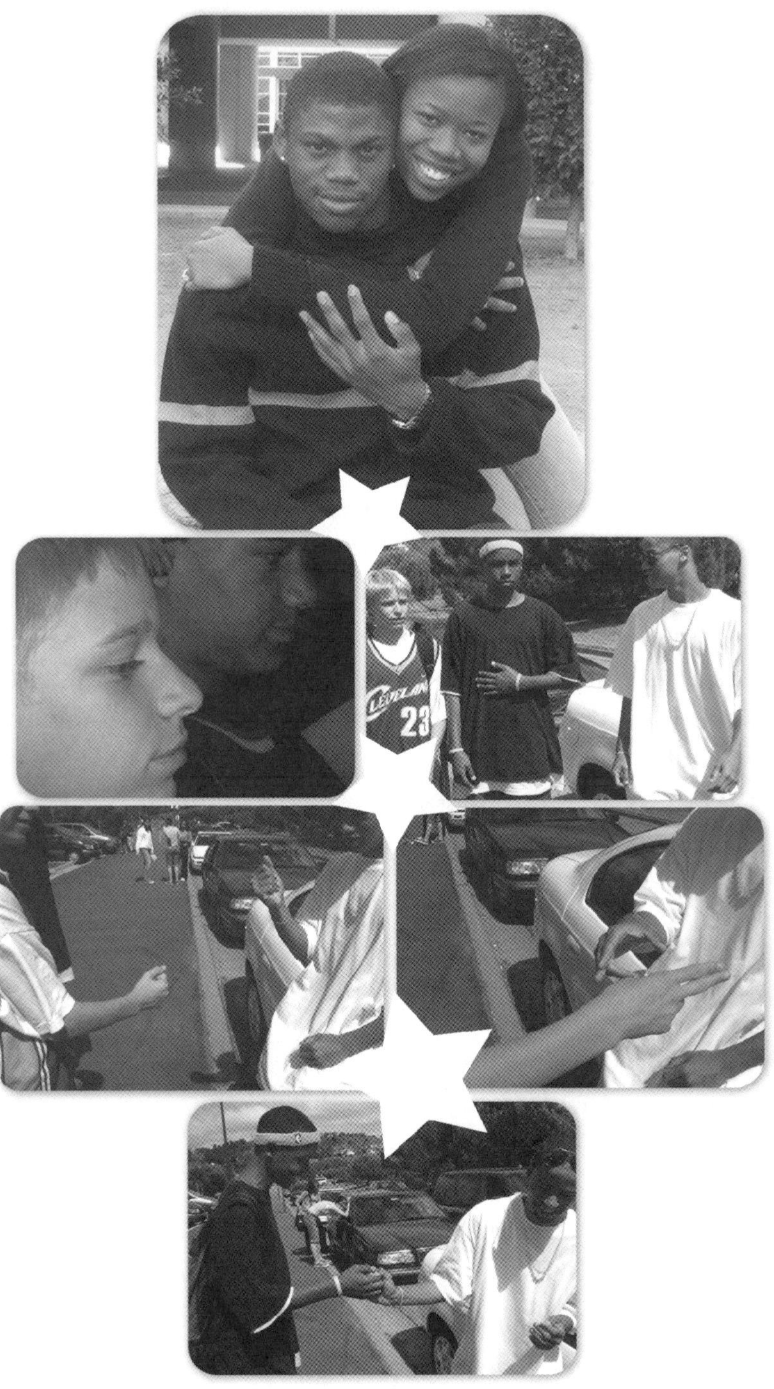

Chapter Four

Steppin' Out: Navigating Your Way in the Real World

*Getting [the] degree meant more to me than an NCAA title,
being named All-American or winning an Olympic Gold Medal.*
—Patrick Ewing

*A tough lesson to learn in life
is that not everybody wishes you well.*
—Dan Rather

If your ship doesn't come in, swim to it!
—Jonathan Winters

You represent 40% of the population and 100% of the future. While the world may be your oyster, it is also counting on you! And because things are better for you than they were for your parents, you have to do MORE.

Your road to adulthood is paved with golden opportunities. It is also booby-trapped with adversity and trials for you to overcome. This chapter focuses on how to navigate your way in the world with success on your radar. It tells you how to develop the where-withal to meet challenges and maximize opportunities. You will put together a navigational chart that helps you dispatch your skills, aptitude, attitude, and smart choices at the harbor of your dreams. The tailwinds of support you get along the way are a plus. But the captain is YOU.

An undisciplined life is an insane life. Today you've got to have some skills or go to college; and better yet, be down with both! Whether it's choppy waters or smooth sailing ahead, character and preparation, not circumstances, determine where and how far you will go. Stepping out means moving into your potential with *no holds barred.* The more you learn and grow as you step out, the more possibilities you will encounter. And the amount of adversity you experience is merely a measure of your greatness.

A Climate of Change, Rapidity and Complexity

The world you are stepping into now is changing fast and it is complicated. Technology is driving much of the change and stepping up the pace of life. Technology also opens the world up and brings it closer to you. With the touch of a button you can 'live' video chat or buy products from the other side of the planet. This is called globalism. Fast paced change and globalism create more possibilities for you. And more possibilities create complexity. Complexity here means that you will deal with various situations on emotional, mental, social and spiritual levels; and usually at the same time. Add today's intense diversity to the mix and you have a lot more complexity. There are many more ways for you to do your life than in your parents' time. There are countless avenues to succeed and prosper, and just as many ways to stumble and fall. In this climate of change, rapidity and complexity you do not have the option to fail. You are required to be astute and focused in almost everything you do, from setting school and career goals, to choosing your friends and associates. This applies whether you are Caucasian, African-American, Hispanic, Asian, male, female or from any social-economic background, class or ability.

Social Challenges

As you enter the world of work and higher education you will also run into some social challenges. These come in the forms of fear, prejudice and small-mindedness. Within teen culture you will come up against peer pressure, sexual temptations and risk. You must be especially aware, focused and savvy to navigate this terrain.

Fear and Other Social Dis-eases

Despite the wondrous achievements of humans, our society has a fierce addiction to fear. It is a major social dis-ease. Fear is *f*alse *e*vidence *a*ppearing *r*eal. And it comes in many forms; some of these are:

- *Fear of success. Fear of failure. Fear of closeness. These all represent fear of Life.*

- *Fear of being authentic—that bad things will happen if one does not think, believe or act in a prescribed way.*

- *Fear of telling the truth. Fear of not having one's way. These represent fear of being annihilated.*

- *Fear that one is helpless and forever victimized by events, people and institutions. This is fear of oneself.*

- *Fear that one is not safe or that one's needs won't be met, and that there is never enough to go around, whatever that may be.*

- *Fear that one is defective or inadequate in some way, and fear that others will find this out.*

- *Fear of the unknown, difference and what one does not understand.*

- *Fear that something is sure to go wrong the moment one relaxes and allows oneself to be happy.*

- *Fear for the sake of fear, because it has become a drug of choice for many people.*

The media and press fuel these fears; employers feed these fears; our social institutions pump up these fears. And so do our egos!

People who attack and prey upon others are driven by these fears. Overdosing on fear reduces a person to indulge in base desires and behaviors, which are aggression, rejection, hatred, pettiness, cynicism, etc. Fearful people of this kind are among the most dangerous on the planet. They will cross your path. And when they do, you can choose to either let them enter your precious circle of life or step away.

Prejudice

At the root of prejudice is fear and small-mindedness. To be prejudiced is to pre-judge others in negative stereotypes and feel justified in treating them poorly. It is a product of fear, which comes from the notion that one's race, lifestyle or cultural stock is superior to others. Prejudice shows up as discrimination, racism, sexism, homophobia, and injustice.

No particular group has the corner on prejudice; it goes all ways. Every race and culture of people displays some form of prejudice. Just as there are Caucasians that hate African-Americans, there are black people who are intensely uncomfortable with white people, and refuse to go around or interact with them. People in general tend to make judgments of others based on stereotypes. It is a human characteristic that we as a civilization have not yet conquered. Its ugly, it hurts and it causes pain.

Small-mindedness

Small-mindedness is just what it implies. It is a cousin of fear. Small-mindedness is walking around with blinders on, refusing to see and acknowledge what is really there in plain view. It is living inside a box and trying to shape the world around one's fears. Small-mindedness, fear and prejudice will not go away. And because you have so much more to work with than your parents' generation, these social dis-eases will be less of an obstruction to your goals, dreams and success.

Today's High Risk Teen Culture

Risk

Teen culture today has an element of risk that is rare. You grow up in a society that glorifies violence and aggression. You grow up in a society that prematurely immerses you in adult sexual images and temptations. These things have an adverse impact on teen culture.

Sex is a sacred act between two people to express their love and devotion and joy. Sex is not something to be played with, and is best experienced in a committed marital relationship; and between people who are emotionally mature, not necessarily physically developed.

The risks from pre-mature and reckless sex can last a lifetime. The chances of becoming infected with diseases such as AIDS, Herpes and other STD's are on the rise among teenagers. Pre-mature sex opens doors for problems, breakdowns, and even early death. It distracts you from what is important. It can consume you. It causes you to grow up too fast, and forfeit your youth before you've had time to enjoy it. Teen pregnancy is absolutely high-risk behavior. We no longer live in a welfare friendly society, and *you* will be responsible to raise that child. You will have to do this in a society where the cost of living is skyrocketing, and where it is easy to become poor and stay poor. Making the choice to grow a baby is taking on a major responsibility that is unnatural for a teenager today. It means that the life you have yet to live is no longer your own.

And their are other risks. In today's teen culture you can lose your life over a petty exchange of words, a pair of shoes, a taco, or if you simply look at someone the wrong way. The fact that more prisons are being built today than schools, testifies to the rise of senseless violence among young people. Low self-esteem, fear and small-mindedness are behind this trend. The choices you make in a moment's desire or from hotheaded recklessness can have ramifications for the rest of your life! With these kinds of risks, it is easier to fall through the cracks and harder to get back up, if you do at all.

Peer Pressure

Within teen culture there is peer pressure. One form is the pressure from other teens who want you to stay as they are, or do as they do in order for them to accept you. And very often, this kind of peer pressure leads to drug use and delinquent behavior. Another kind of teen peer pressure comes from those who lay a guilt-trip on you as you make choices to better your self. They are threatened by your goals and do not want you to become better than them. And then there is the peer pressure that comes from those who resent you because you are different or stand out in a special way. They put you down, make fun of you, tease or wonder why you are the way you are. This is known as the "barrel full of monkeys" syndrome. Peer pressure of this kind stunts your growth and holds you back if you give in to it. People who come at you this way want your power and your energy. They can make the same choices as you to better themselves. But they choose not to do so.

Fear and the risks and pressures of teen culture are not insurmountable. Stepping over and around them builds character and spurs you onward to higher ground.

The Power of Education

You can lose your car, a home, your clothes; you can lose all your worldly possessions. But no one can take away your education. That is yours for keeps.

If you don't do some things to prepare your self there is only so far that you can go. Education is the primary way that you prepare to meet and navigate your way in the real world.

According to current government statistics:

- *High school dropouts are 72% more likely to be unemployed.*
- *Dropouts earn 27% less than high school graduates.*
- *Dropouts are three times as likely to face poverty and receive public assistance than are high school graduates.*
- *Approximately 45% of prisoners are dropouts.*

Knowledge is the new currency. Knowledge comes from education. Not completing a high school education or going on to college are bad choices today. This is especially true if you want to succeed in business. A high school diploma or GED is essential. Once you've done that, you need a Bachelors degree. And because most of the people who will compete for jobs have a Bachelors degree, you want to seriously consider going up the ladder for a Masters degree.

Education not only enables you to qualify for jobs or get you through the corporate door, it strengthens you and gives you advantages in other ways. A college education helps to groom you for entrepreneurial work. It expands your vision of what is possible for you. The learning you get from a college education naturally trains you to work with other people, to problem-solve, to think independently, and to discipline your self. From it you get exposure to opportunities and resources. Getting an education is one of the most loving and healthy things you can do for your self.

What are colleges looking for?

Veronica Leigh Taylor graduated with honors from Hampton University in 1999. Her Bachelors degree is in broadcast journalism. She is an African-American who worked in a major corporation while pursuing her Masters degree. Veronica volunteers with a community organization that helps young people with employment skills and college preparation. She has now advanced her career to play a key role in public service. According to Veronica, colleges today are looking more closely at two things to qualify you for college acceptance and entry: They are the SAT (Standard Aptitude Test) scores and GPA (Grade Point Average). These are the primary criteria that will determine your qualification to enter most colleges today, not your race, sex or economic background. You must therefore take these seriously.

Veronica advises that key steps for preparing for college are to:
1.   Improve your writing skills.

2. Take a SAT prep course during your sophomore year of high school.

3. Start collecting college applications the summer before beginning your senior year of high school.

4. Submit your college applications before Thanksgiving of your senior year of high school. For early admission, submit applications before October 1st.

What about the cost?

Don't let the cost of going to college discourage you. The cost will more than likely be outweighed by the bounty of benefits, opportunities and growth you will gain from a college education. One way to cut costs is to attend a Jr. College for a few years and then move onto a 4-year college to complete your degree. Some teens work their way through college with part-time jobs. Learn through your school about financial aid programs, grants or scholarships. Remember, something that cannot be taken away from you should be valued as priceless!

Education is Freedom

Education expands you. It opens your eyes and lets you see better what is going on around you. It sharpens your senses, and it helps you to become an independent and responsible thinker. It frees you from the traps of shallowness and small-mindedness. Education opens many doors. Don't let friends or family members guilt-trip you into feeling that education is a cope-out. Don't allow them to make you feel that you are betraying them by pursuing a good and higher education. Even they know the power of learning, and how it can change you. No one benefits by you playing small or compromising your goals in order to please others! Your education can enable you to help them grow.

Work and Career

The world of work is not the one that existed in your parents' generation. Working at the same job for most of your life is almost a thing of the past. Today, it is normal to have several jobs that last an average of 2 years each, during your career. That is because of the rampant change in organizations.

In the world of work you enter, 60% of jobs will be permanent part-time, and without benefits. This means that you will not have one full-time job, but two or three, depending on your financial needs. You must navigate this world and make it *work* for you.

What are employers looking for?

1. *Professionalism*. You need to be able to fit into the company's culture. Organizations want people who dress appropriately and communicate well. This means that the language you use with friends is not the language you use at work. Veronica Leigh Taylor shared with me a story about a young man who was hired into a corporation and showed up one day and said "what's up ma nigga" to a co-worker. This did not go over very well, even to the co-worker, who was also African-American. And then there was the young woman who showed up for work wearing a skirt so tight that you could see her butt cheek. She was sent home.

   Adapting to a company's culture does not mean that you lose your self or 'kiss-up'. It means that you become wise and savvy on how to "show up" properly. Here you must equip your self with the right etiquette and protocols to deal with many kinds of people in many kinds of situations, and on local, national and international levels.

2. *Writing Skills.* The ability to write letters, reports or other forms of communication is of great importance in organizations. This includes email! Take your English and Literature courses seriously.

3. *Service-orientation.* Many young people today have a sense of entitlement. This means that they don't want to apply themselves, yet they expect things to magically come to them. They don't feel that they have to pay any dues. Spoiled, is the word here. This attitude will end a job and send you packing fast! Employers want people who are outgoing and see themselves as part of a community. They want to see you joining civic organizations and doing outreach or volunteer work. This is because many organizations have community outreach goals and initiatives they need to meet. Being willing to help others is a big value to today's businesses. You will be expected to maintain a network of public and professional groups, and to give more service than you are paid for.

4. *Team Player and Attitude.* In the workplace you will naturally work with people. You will be expected to team up on projects with other people on a regular basis. The employer wants you to put on your 'game face' and join the team. It does not want you to be about drama or be a conflict instigator. It wants you to be comfortable getting involved with others instead of avoiding them.

   You will be expected to express your thoughts and opinions, exchange ideas, and take directions. You will be required to be adaptable and flexible to changing situations and multiple tasks. Good speaking and listening skills are required here, as well as a good attitude.

5. *Multi-cultural Skills.* The world is rapidly becoming highly diverse, and so is the workplace. Organizations want you to be able to deal with different kinds of people and in various situations. You will be expected to know a foreign language (Hispanic or Asian), and you will be expected to know something about other peoples' customs. This knowledge will become a part of your work style.

6. *Creativity.* Employers seek people who bring something to the table. This includes coming up with new ideas and approaches, innovating and problem solving. They want you to 'let it rip'. Your ability to do this raises your value in any work situation.

7. *Technical Skills.* Did you notice that this is the last item on this list? The reason is that in the workplace your technical skills account for about 15% of your overall qualifications. All of the other items listed above represent 85% of what makes you qualified and a desirable employee. This is where many young people make the mistake of believing that their talent and skills alone will bring them what they want or help them get by. Nothing could be further from the truth!

Internships

Many corporations have internships that allow you to work in a business environment while going to school, and get paid for it! You can learn about these through your high school, by contacting large corporations, or researching them at a library. Doing an internship is an excellent way to get early exposure and training in the business world.

Being an Entrepreneur

There is no such thing as a stable, guaranteed job today. Often, the best employment option is to work for your self. This can give you greater security and freedom than being an employee. But it also has its challenges. Being your own boss requires a firm vision, discipline, planning, organization and focus. It requires the ability to deal with many kinds of people. Being your own boss can be a lot more work than being an employee. But it is worth it.

Many young people are pursuing this option. There are many productive ways to do this. While he was a freshman at Texas Southern University, my nephew Gregory saw an opportunity and began selling used books to fellow college students. His book business grew and paid some of his college expenses. Now a graduate of TSU,

Gregory has grown this into a full-fledged book selling enterprise, and housed on its own real estate!

While you may spend some time working for a corporation, owning your own business is something to consider as doable. In fact, you are functioning as an entrepreneur whether you work for your self or an organization. This is because in both cases, you must continually be on the lookout for openings that will take you to the next level in your career. You must see your job as a vehicle to develop certain strengths, talents and skills, and that gives you exposure to other opportunities. It means taking responsibility for your growth by choosing those jobs that connect with your goals and vision.

The Black Star Project * is an organization of professionals that mentors and motivates teens to achieve academic excellence and career focus.

Spirit Rising

Yours is a generation set apart from all others. Just as the baby boomer and generation X impacted our society in a unique way, yours is the *Indigo* * generation, which is about bringing greater peace and spirit into the world. Much of what your generation experiences rides on a spiritual beam, in terms of school, work and personal and social lives. Teens of your generation are abundantly gifted and have the genius to master their lives and achieve fantastic things at an earlier rate than most adults. They have the capacity to foster healing and community, and to be natural leaders. Your generation is fit for today's times!

There is a higher plan for your life that is greater than your problems or the challenges you will meet on your path. The rise of spirit in the world today is a call for wisdom and personal nobility, for people to treat themselves and one another better. It means that people have an urgent desire to experience peace, purpose, joy and a relationship with the sacred in their work and personal lives. The

50

rampant fear in the world is a cry for people to return to the source, which is love and trust in the life process. The work and service you provide as a teen and adult can help to usher in this spirit. This does not mean that you should try to change the world. But you can make a serious dent!

☙ ❧ ☙ ❧ ☙ ❧

What You Can Do

The *Navigational Skills* you will need in the real world are:

1. Self-knowledge.

A basic sense of self-knowledge is a requirement for success in school and work. This knowledge consists of an understanding of your goals, vision, strengths, weaknesses and gifts. It is an awareness of the parts of your self that help you, and those parts that get you into trouble.

2. Positive Attitude.

Attitude is 97% of life. How you choose to meet and respond to situations is *attitude*. A chip on your shoulder will only bring poor results and rejection. A good attitude is about being a problem-solver, not part of the problem. Good attitude is about being discreet, diplomatic and kind.

3. A Healthy Body.

A healthy body is central to all that you do. Not much is going to happen without it. Simple advice: Put good things into your body and do good things to it. Good health gives you a shine and helps to promote you.

4. A Skill or Talent that is Marketable.

Your skill is something you acquire as a result of practice or training in an art, profession or craft such as computer skills, architectural skills, or teaching skills. These are also called trades or 'technical skills', which comes from the word 'technique' or how you do something. These skills can be acquired through internships, apprenticeships, job training or experience, or trade schools. A talent is your natural ability or power—something you do well and enjoy. Skill and talent have value and form your overall personal package. Both are marketable and important to employment or running your own business.

5. Goal Oriented.

Before a building can be constructed, there must first be a blueprint. A ship cannot sail to a final destination without a navigational chart. In order for you to reach your goals you must have a plan. Most people who have achieved something significant in their lives worked with a plan. A goal inspires activity in your life, which generates momentum. Applying your self towards achieving goals also helps you to discover what you do best and what you enjoy doing.

Your goals will change many times in life; however, the basic approach to achieving them does not. A goal-setting guide is provided in Appendix A.

6. Discipline.

You must be organized, focused, and take responsibility for your choices while practicing restraint and discernment. Discipline means weighing the pros and cons of a situation before you choose how to approach it.

Discipline means keeping your goals in sight, and not allowing your self to become distracted by reckless or counterproductive behavior. In this way, you will be poised and ready to go through the doors that open up to you. It is better to be prepared and not have an opportunity than to have an opportunity and not be prepared for it.

7. Good Communication and People Skills.

Communication and people skills are standards by which anyone's competence and intelligence are measured, regardless of race, culture or background. You must value and be able to speak and write in the language learned in school, and that everyone understands. You must be able to interact with people in a constructive manner and build collaborative relationships.

The ability to communicate with various people in a variety of situations is one of the most powerful tools you can possess. The first impression people have of you is how you talk and express your self. And first impressions are hard to change.

You will be required to speak clearly, directly, and confidently. Public speaking courses can help you develop this skill. When you speak well, you command respect.

People skill is interacting with others to achieve favorable outcomes. These are also called 'interpersonal skills'. It means listening and being sensitive to other people's points of view, but not necessarily compromising your own. It is minimizing conflict between your self and others. Some basic ways to manage conflict are listed in Appendix C.

8. Being Proactive, Assertive and Persistent.

Being *proactive* means making things happen rather than letting things happen to you. It is anticipating future needs and changes in your life and planning ways to address them. This requires initiative and directing your life responsibly. It means taking the long view and making plans that will benefit you in the present and future.

For example: You may be graduating from high school in a year. What will you do then? Should you be researching and applying for colleges now or planning to take a job? If you plan to get a job, what kind of job will it be? What kind of preparation do you need? Are there corporate internships you can pursue? Do you wish to see the world and have an independent life before working or getting married? Should you find out about college transfer programs now that will allow you to travel? How much money will you need and how will you acquire it? And if you decide to travel, work or go to college, is it a good idea to get pregnant now? These are proactive questions you need to ask your self. They help you to plan your life realistically and carefully.

Being *assertive* is not to be confused with being aggressive, nor egotistical. Being assertive is broadcasting your dreams—asking for what you want, putting it out there for all to see and know. No one will know who you are, what you want to do, or what you do well unless you broadcast it. This does not mean bragging. Nor is it to be confused with the idea that other people owe you something—they do not. Broadcasting your dreams is honoring your vision and talent and wanting to give them to the world. Community leaders, school officials or people working in a field that you want to pursue can help to give your vision legs to walk and wings to fly. In order for things to gravitate your way, you must make your self visible.

Persistence means to honor your goals by continuing to seek what is required to achieve them. It is asking for help, not because you are weak, but because you are strong. And it is because you know you deserve the help you are seeking. Persistence is not being afraid of 'NO'. Most people are so negative that they have to say no several times before they can say "yes". So keep on asking until you get to "YES".

9. Global Perspective.
Often teens become easily seduced into counterproductive behavior when their world is too small. Many teens never venture beyond their immediate home and school environments. They see the world through the TV screen or other people's eyes. This is extremely limiting and a risky way to live today. Renowned motivational speaker, Les Brown, calls this a 'hood infected virus' or (HIV), which is the dead-end life and shallowness that results from keeping your world small.

It is imperative that you expand your world and expose your self to different kinds of people and life enhancing experiences. Teen life is not meant to be about sex, drugs and hanging out. This rich time should not be squandered but explored with wonder!

Being expansive and exposing your self to different peoples' ways of doing things reduces the anger you may feel from racism, sexism and other 'isms' in the world. This does not make these dis-eases OK, but being expansive makes you keener in your ability to respond in ways that won't trip you up or set you back. With the insight that comes from exposure, you are more intelligent and your response to 'isms' is less ruled by haste or emotion. You can appreciate how people are more similar than they are different. A global perspective helps you see your self as an important part of the human community, despite what people may feel about your race, culture or lifestyle.

The world is your stage! Living globally is living large and taking your show on the road. It is having the moxie to taste the many flavors of life; to reach beyond what you even thought was possible to achieve; and to command the admiration and respect that is your due for your good works.

10. Ability to Network

You need people and they need you. You must be able to maintain a network of professional and community organizations. You must be able to take advantage of the connections through people that are always there, and tap into resources to support your career goals. Networking is give and take. Constructive interpersonal skills help you to develop and maintain your network.

Your network determines your net worth. So you must use good judgment to surround your self with people who support your vision and nurture your gifts. People in your career and professional network may not always be close friends, and that is OK. Sometimes this is better, because it keeps healthy boundaries. But you can still have harmonious relationships with them.

11. Diversity Appreciation.

Fear and rejection of difference is a major handicap in today's world. You must have a genuine comfort and willingness to embrace other peoples' differences, just as you expect them to embrace your own. Being able to converse in a foreign language will put you at an advantage. So will your knowledge of other cultural traditions. More opportunities are available to you when you open up to diversity. In addition to work and school activities, it benefits you to include people of differing backgrounds and customs as friends. This includes 'physically challenged' people. By doing so you learn from them and they learn from you. You begin to appreciate the problems and needs everyone has in common as human beings.

12. Emotional Intelligence.

Because you will be interfacing with people at school and work you will be expected to manage your emotions. School and work are not the best arenas to play out your feelings. This can lead to conflict or problems. Emotional intelligence means not being ruled by your impulses, but balancing feelings with facts. It means to avoid taking things personally, and to avoid making assumptions about people's behavior. It is applying your good people skills to check things out before responding to adverse situations.

When it comes to racism, you will do better not to obsess about it. It is out there, both behind the scenes and in your face. You must be aware but not paranoid about it. When you look for racism you see it everywhere. When you concentrate on racism it will come running to you. And when you must confront the racism that even the blind can see, you can rely upon your good people skills, not your emotions, to work the situation. This applies to other forms of personal affronts you may experience.

13. Lifelong Learning.

Because change is a constant, you will always be impacted by it. In order to have a positive relationship with change you must be a lifelong learner. You must view your self as continuing your education well beyond high school and college. You must approach the challenges and problems you encounter as courses and tests, and the people you meet along the way as teachers who keep you growing. When you stop learning you stop growing.

14. Commitment to Excellence.

Bringing your "A" game to everything you do is the mark of excellence. You are now competing against many people who want the same things as you. But that is not the only reason to commit to excellence. Your best will change from one day to the next, from one task to another. It is the *act* of doing your best that makes you feel good. And when you do your best and know it, other people know this too.

15. Reverence for a Higher Spiritual Power.

Reverence for a Higher Spiritual Power is at the center of a balanced life. All that you do and that happens to you is in relation to and in service of the Divine. Wisdom is acknowledging and honoring this truth.

Ego is 'edging God out'. What you do is not all about you. With your gifts, talent and skill, you are an instrument of a Divine will. Aligning your self with this spirit and living by its laws is your truest source of security, peace and success in today's dynamic world.

And remember that people come to know God in many ways. Because we live in a diverse world, people come to know the Higher Spiritual Power according to their own customs and traditions. But all ways connect us to spirit—that universal, creative power that governs all life. And that is what really matters.

** Indigo Children—(For information go to Google.com)*
**The Black Start Project. Blackstarproject.org*

Chapter Five

Straight Up!
Taking Charge of Your Life

*You either cut the mustard or had mustard
smeared all over your sorry face.*
—Ray Charles

*Good is everything that promotes and increases the life force;
bad is everything that hampers and lessens it.*
—African Oral Tradition

Self-preservation is the first law of nature.
—Samuel Butler

This chapter is about personal mastery. It helps you to look at ways to better understand and govern your inner world of thoughts, beliefs, feelings and programming. It helps you find ways to bring out your best, and to minimize the ways you can betray your self. You have within you both, the capacity for greatness and the potential for utter evil, failure and destruction. Character is measured by the ability to manage internal demons while promoting your truest self.

With the many challenges you face, it is easy to understand how you could throw up your hands and say, *"Okay, I give up, I won't even try."* A positive sense of self can be hard to maintain. Evil and self-destruction set in when young people like you, are most vulnerable.

Self-Respect—Self-Love

Self-respect and self-love are flip sides of the same coin. Personal mastery begins with a fierce love and respect for your self. Self-respect is to consider and hold your self in high regard. It means to treat your self properly and dutifully, and not to intrude upon your own best interests. Respect energizes and helps, disrespect de-energizes and harms. No one has the right to disrespect you, not even you! To do this is a violation of your own personal code of honor. In order to master your self you must respect your self. You show self-respect in many ways: Respect for your mind, respect for your body, and respect for your circle of life. You respect what you feel, and what you bring to the table. Your journey into adulthood and your will to learn and grow deserves your respect.

Self-love is a genuine appreciation for your own life and for being alive. Self-love is not to be confused with being "in love" with your self, ego, nor vanity. You demonstrate self-love by taking care of your self emotionally, physically, mentally and spiritually; and by taking care of your responsibilities to your self—as well as others. Self-love is also the act of trusting your self. It is trusting that you are fundamentally good; and trusting that you deserve to do your best, be your best, and to enjoy all which flows from that. When you love your self, you can love others. Self-love propels you to take charge of your life.

Taming the Villain Within

Like a beast lurking in the closet, you have your own villain inside your mind. Your mental villain wants to ambush your dreams. This is a moody, ill-tempered fiend who crusades about in your head, cursing all that is positive about you and that supports your growth. This trifling little fiend speaks the language of doubt, shame, hate, anger, fear and ignorance.

The villain within has a lot to say and relentlessly puts it to your ear. It tells you that you are unworthy and have no personal value; that you have nothing the world can use. It tells you that the negative things other people think and say about you are true. It tells you that you don't deserve to have your needs met or to have a productive, healthy or prosperous life. It tries to convince you that you are weak, that you are a victim of other people's abuse, and therefore, you do not have to take responsibility for your self. This villain tells you that you cannot think for your self and that you should allow your peers to think for you. This villain tells you to harm your self: To do drugs, to debase your body—to get criminal. It glorifies pettiness and idleness and tells you to do the same. It tells you that life is hell and to distrust new experiences. It tells you that people in general, are there for you to use; and that you are strong when you are cynical, cold-hearted and when you show an angry face to the world.

The villain within is on a mission to destroy you, to see you fail by becoming like it. It is your worst enemy and must be stopped!

Unleashing the Champion Within

Your public champions are people who had the courage to make a good thing of their lives. You have that same star quality within you. The champion is the side of your self that believes in you and wants to help you achieve your potential and succeed. Your champion within fights valiantly for you. It is your defender, protector and supporter. It speaks the language of possibility, trust and open-mindedness, kindness, purpose and joy. The champion reminds you of your gifts and uniqueness that can benefit many. It tells you that you are worthy of love and respect, and how to respect your body and mind. It tells you who to choose as friends, and who will nurture and support you. The champion urges you to be patient, wise, disciplined and confident— to do the right thing. The champion keeps you on track and focused. With the champion, you stay honest; you stay true to your self.

The champion's voice is softer, and sometimes can't get a word in because the villain tends to dominate the space. But the champion's mission is to help you to rise and experience the life that is your birthright. It is your best friend. Tune into and unleash the champion within.

You Choose!

At age 14 teens begin to have the kinds of experiences that require them to make choices that will have lasting impact in their lives. This is the time to begin doing what you are *supposed* to do, rather than what you want to do. Whether you heed the demands of the villain or the wisdom of the champion is up to you. The one you feed is a *choice* that you make!

A choice is the power, right, liberty and option to select. And taking charge of your life means to do this with care. You choose what you think, what you believe, how you respond to situations and what actions you will take. Period! Even when you are at your lowest moment, and when you are most challenged, you are never deprived of your power to make a choice—to choose something. This is something that nothing or no one can take away from you. And it makes you ultimately responsible for your behavior and your own life.

You can never, NOT be making a choice. Even when you think you are not making a choice, you are!

Teen life is the time when you increasingly own everything you do. A common trap that teens fall into is making negative choices in reaction to someone else's bad choice. And then they are surprised when the outcomes of their own choice comes back to kick them in the butt. *For example:* If you choose to cop an attitude and tune out on a class because you have a problem with the teacher, whom do you think the consequences will impact? The failing grade that will result from your choice certainly won't affect the teacher or your classmates.

Being accountable is to understand that you are responsible for the choices and decisions you generate, regardless of how irresponsible other people's choices may be. Your choices are not forced upon you by other people's behavior, nor are they determined by the conditions of your life. Family history, race, or education have nothing to do with how you behave. You decide how you are going to think and act. You decide to cut a class, do drugs, harm someone, or give in to peer pressure, because that is what you want to do, not because everyone else is doing these things; and not because somebody made you do it.

Both traits—the villain and champion—will always be with you. This is a simple fact of human nature. Everyone has the capacity for both good and evil; however, the voice that you listen to and allow to guide you will be the one that will run your life. The more you heed the bidding of the villain, the more non-productive and negative your life will be. The more you follow the guidance of the champion, the richer and more progressive your life and experiences will become.

You can't get away from your shadow. When you choose to follow the wisdom of the champion you must also decide how you are going to tame the villain within.

Roger's story

Roger is a 17 year-old African-American teen. He came into one of my youth workshops very late one day, complaining that it was the bus driver's fault. I asked Roger to explain. He said that on the bus he was taking, the bus driver 'got in his face' and made him mad. It started when he asked the driver a question about the route. Then the driver shouted back at Roger, saying that he was holding up the people trying to get on the bus with his questions and told him to sit down. Roger said that this made him mad, so he shouted back at the driver. The driver then ordered Roger off the bus, and he had to wait for another one. That is why he was late. After Roger shared his story, I asked him some questions. This is how the exchange went:

Dr. Taylor—So how is your being late the bus driver's fault?

Roger—Because he got in my face man, and 'dissed' me in front of all those people, and didn't answer my question. He made me mad so I got back in his face.

Dr. Taylor—So he got into your mind and told you to get mad?

Roger—No, it's not like that. He just made me mad.

Dr. Taylor—How did he make you mad? Did he tell you to get mad?

Roger—No. I don't know.

Dr. Taylor—OK, so you "dissed him back" because you were mad?

Roger—Yeah, I wouldn't have if he hadn't made me mad. I called him some names and then he up and told me to get off the bus. I had to wait for another one. That's why I'm late.

Dr. Taylor—So after you got mad who told you to call the bus driver names?

Roger—He made me do it because he "pissed" me off!

Dr. Taylor—So you decided to call him names.

Roger—Yeah. I decided that if he disses on me I'll diss on him back so he can see how it feels.

Dr, Taylor—So how can the person who made you decide to call him names be different from the one who told you to get mad?

Roger—I don't know. I guess it was me.

Dr. Taylor—So the bus driver did not say to you, "Roger, get mad and call me names."

Roger—No, I guess not, I guess I did.

Dr. Taylor—Would you say that the outcome of both of those choices was you being thrown off the bus?

Roger—Yeah, I guess so.

Dr. Taylor—So if you could have fore seen the consequence of choosing to get mad and calling him names, what other choice could you have made in that moment?

Roger—I could have just ignored that man. I could've said, "You got it bro", and moved on to a seat.

Dr. Taylor—The bus driver was wrong, and he did not know anything about you, did he?

Roger—No. He was just trippin'. I wasted my time on his ass.

Dr. Taylor—So, whose fault is it that you are late today?

Roger—I guess it's mine.

Dr. Taylor—So can you see that no one makes you mad or act in a certain way, that is a choice you make?

Roger—Yeah, I see that now. That's some pretty deep stuff.

Dr. Taylor—Roger, thank you for teaching us something today about choices. And Roger, can you say a private 'thank you' to that bus driver for giving you a very important lesson?

Roger—Yeah, I can do that.

What You Can Do

1. Confront the villain within.

You must search your self and admit that you may carry self-defeating attitudes and beliefs about your self, and about life in general. Ask your self, *"What do I dislike about myself? What kind of negative thoughts, beliefs, and attitudes do I entertain in my mind? Where I do I get these thoughts and beliefs?"* List the things about your personality that get you into trouble, and that you feel you can and should change. Decide how you are going to change these things. Put a time schedule to it. Make this a personal growth goal.

2. Embrace the champion within.

Search your self and acknowledge the wholesome attitudes and beliefs about your self, and about life that will support your growth. Ask your self, *"What do I like about myself? What kinds of positive thoughts, attitudes and beliefs do I entertain in my mind? Why do I think and believe these things?"* List the personality strengths that are working for you. Decide how you will build on your strengths.

3. Watch what you say to your self.

You talk to your self more than you talk to anyone else. Think about that. What you say about your self in your private mind becomes true, both the good and the bad. Learn to monitor the conversations in your mind and the opinions you hold about your self. Learn to distinguish between what people think about you, and what you think about your self. This includes your friends, family and authority figures.

Make it a habit to replace negative thoughts about your self with positive ones. Quiet the villain and let the champion speak. *For example,* avoid these kinds of thoughts: *"I'm so fat. I never do anything right. People don't like me. I'll fail if I try. I can't read well. I hate math—it's too hard for me".* Say instead, *"I am an attractive person. People respect and appreciate me because I respect and appreciate myself. I am becoming successful. I approach my activities with confidence. I am in the process of improving my reading and math skills."* Replace limiting phrases with power affirmations. Rather than saying, *"I am trying to succeed."* Say, *"I am in the process of succeeding."* And *"I will or I won't"* instead of, *"I can't."* The more you positively affirm your self, the better you feel and you grow your self-esteem. (See the Step-by-Step Guide to Building High Self-Esteem in Appendix B of this book.)

4. Don't be a victim. Don't be a toy.

Victims are toys. They get played with. It is a bad habit, a hazard and a deadly trap. Wallowing in self-pity may be a warm and easy thing to do, but it strips you of your dignity and makes you vulnerable to abuse.

Victims are in the habit of feeling forever, persecuted. In the victim's mind, someone is always out to get them. You can count on victims to have a sorry story to tell. Victims insist that 'somebody' owes them something. In their world, everybody is wrong and they are right. Victims blame others for their own weaknesses, problems and failures. And they hardly ever, take responsibility for their own choices and behaviors. Victims whine when they cannot have their way. And even when they do, they are not satisfied. These behaviors are for children, not teenagers and adults.

Believing that you are a victim is one of the most lethal impediments to your growth. What you are really doing when you become the victim is to victimize your self through your own miserable beliefs, thoughts and attitudes. When you proclaim to the world that you are victimized by someone else's behavior, or that you are a victim of circumstances, you give up your power to control your destiny. You toss it up for grabs, and become a pawn in someone else's game. And when you do this you have seriously harmed your life. Remember this.

Choose not to be a victim. Whenever you feel tempted to feel like a victim, say to your self instead, *"I am in control of my life. I am unfolding in joy. I have many options and resources available to me. The difficulties I face are a temporary setback, and I am in the process of making responsible choices to overcome them. I may not have a lot, but I am workin' what I've got!"*

5. Turn the anger into something else.

As a teen you may carry anger around for some reason. It could be from childhood wounds, abuse, unfairness, or inherited from someone close to you. Yes, anger can be inherited, because it is contagious. Anger blurs your vision and causes you to wobble and stumble. You cannot stay clear or focused with anger in your mind and heart. Anger causes you to make poor choices that can hurt your life. And you are better than that.

Anger is its own reward. As long as you hate, you will have something to hate. Realize that anger is negative energy that can only bring about perverse results. It produces pain, frustration, conflict, suffering, defeat and more anger. The one thing that your anger will ultimately destroy is you. So stop letting the anger deal with you. Deal with it! Single out its source. Did you take it on from parents, or someone else? Is there an unresolved painful issue that keeps the anger alive within you? Find its nest and choose to shake loose from its spell.

And then, be intelligent. Turn the anger into something else. Use it for creative and vital purposes. Direct this energy into something that will lift you up. Turn it into determination and a fierce search for self-knowledge and wisdom. Turn it into passion and compassion. Take it to a higher level. Turn it into a dream. Begin now.

6. Share your feelings.

What you feel is important. Whether it is joy or anger, confidence or defeat. When sad, hard feelings are pinned up inside, they fester and become more intense. They eat away at you, which can affect your health. Feelings are energy, and this energy has to go somewhere. Share them with someone you trust and who will respect your emotions—someone who will sit down and listen to you, wholeheartedly. Someone who will let you speak without rebuttal or judgment—someone who will hear you. This is important. Sharing your feelings is the beginning of resolving them.

7. Dismiss other people's negative stuff.

Understand that what others think of you have more to do with how they have been programmed. Their opinion of you should not shape your reality. People's beliefs and attitudes may be unhealthy for you and contaminating. Their attitudes reflect their problems and hang-ups, and have little or nothing to do with you. Just as you would not eat anything someone hands to you, learn to be selective about what thoughts, beliefs, and attitudes you take on. (See the Step-by-Step Guide to Building High Self-Esteem in Appendix B of this book).

Zoe's story

Zoe is a 15 year-old Caucasian. She is an "A" student, her mother tells me. However, Zoe's mother is quite concerned for Zoe's emotional welfare. It appears that while she gets good grades, Zoe is teased about her weight by other girls at her school. The daily teasing is so unbearable for Zoe that she spends her lunch hours in the girls' bathroom sitting on the toilet set cover with the stall door closed and locked. She goes there to avoid being attacked, and to be alone to read and study. She feels safe there. I advised Zoe's mother to tell her the following: That the teasing is a result of the other girls' jealousy, who are trying to pull Zoe into their zone. It is peer pressure for Zoe not to excel in school because her excellence threatens them. Zoe needs to understand that the teasing are only words and cannot hurt her. It is what she chooses to believe about herself that will do this. Zoe can choose to feel flattered that these girls are spending so much time and energy on her—giving her so much of their attention. I advised Zoe's mother to report the harassment to a school official, and to have Zoe speak to a school counselor, and to recommend counseling for the girls who are teasing Zoe. Zoe needs to come out of the bathroom stall, to be her 'self' and to wish the girls who tease her growth.

8. Choose your friends and associations wisely.

Outside school and work you choose 100% of the time, the people who will make up your circle of friends and associates. Whether you call them your 'homies', your crew, squad or posse, the people you bring into your circle of life are a direct reflection of how you feel about your self. These are some of the most important choices you make in your journey.

You choose your friends. Even when people approach you first, you decide whether to enter into a friendship with them. Remember, your enemies also choose you. People with low self-esteem have little or no regard for themselves, and that is why they cannot genuinely care about you. Do no expect them to. Distance your self from them and wish them growth. Trust your instincts. Do not bring 'questionable' persons into your precious circle of life. If they don't feel right, don't go there. They may or may not be 'bad' people, but in either case, the choices they make can adversely affect you.

The people you choose will strongly influence your quality of life. They will determine the amount of pain, joy, conflict or peace you will have. Respect your circle of life. Choose those who have a healthy attitude for themselves, like you. Choose those who are positively motivated and that treat you well. You want and need people around you who build you up not tear you down.

Isaiah's Story

Isaiah and Jordan, both 15 years old, had been friends since 5th grade. Jordan is Caucasian and Isaiah is bi-racial, with a German and Asian heritage. Their friendship had a rocky beginning because Jordan bullied Isaiah around. In the playground, Jordan would hit Isaiah and take things away from him. This bullying ended when Isaiah struck Jordan back, knocking him to the ground. Since then, Jordan and Isaiah were 'friends'. They continued to hang out in high school. After school and on weekends they played video games, hung out at the mall or played basketball. Isaiah began to notice that Jordan was getting into a lot of trouble both at school and with his parents, and he was grounded a lot. One day Isaiah's parents received a call from a police officer investigating the theft of a cell phone. He caught Jordan who had stolen the phone, but Jordan told the police officer that he sold the phone to Isaiah. Jordan lied to the police because he was afraid and did not want to turn the phone over to him. So he recklessly incriminated his 'friend'. Isaiah and his parents firmly told the police that Isaiah had nothing to do with the stolen cell phone. And because Jordan was growing his reputation as a problem teen, the police believed their story over Jordan's lies.

This incident made Isaiah realize that Jordan was not a real friend and that he would no longer hang out with him. The call from the police really frightened Isaiah, and he did not want to be pulled into something like that again.

9. Wish them growth.

Teasing, harassing and bullying are behaviors that come from people who have a low opinion of themselves. They have their challenges also, perhaps greater than your own. Remember that people who attack and offend you out of their prejudices and small-mindedness have to grow beyond their limitations. Possibly their biggest hurdle is to overcome their insecurity, low self-esteem, fear and ignorance.

Don't take their hate or fear into your own heart. You have a strong advantage over these kinds of people when you decide not to react to their problems, or be consumed by their drama, and instead, to wish them growth. When you wish the people who offend you growth, the positive energy you send out to them circles back and it blesses you!

10. Adopt a mentor or personal coach.

Whether you are on target or straying from your path, spirit will send you support to help you grow. Often this comes in the form of people who enter your life to give you just the inspiration or assistance you need at that time. These people are like guardian angels. Most people today benefit from having a personal coach. Just as people require a fitness trainer to help them strengthen their bodies in the gym, a personal coach is someone who tells you what they see in you, and how you can keep unfolding.

Often other people see beauty, goodness and potential within you that you don't see. They can help you harvest and bring these out. You can always benefit from the guidance of someone else in your journey. Open up and take the hand of someone who really has your best interest in mind—someone you trust and someone who believes in you. This could be a family member, teacher, a community leader, a neighbor or close friend. Two heads are usually better than one.

11. Consider the source of the advice you get.

When people offer you advice, be they adults, authority figures, or friends, always take a good look at their character. How do they live their lives? Do they make responsible choices? How do their personal examples hold up? Do they follow their own advice? And do they have your best interest at heart? Ask your self these questions before taking their word. And when you do follow someone's advice, remember that the decision to do this is a choice made by *you*.

12. Keep your vehicle in optimal condition.

You can change many cars over a lifetime. But your physical body is the only vehicle that will carry you through your journey. How you care for it today will affect how it will function years from now.

Drugs and AIDS damage and destroy many teen lives. An intelligent person regards his and her body with great affection; practices common sense and moderation; and considers the consequences of any activity involving his or her physical welfare.

Taking charge of your life means taking care of your body. Try not to go to extremes where your desires are concerned. Respect your body. Be mindful of what you put into it, and what you do with it. Understand that true manhood and womanhood does not come with biological maturity; it is earned by living a responsible life. And there are no better highs or pleasures than the ones you get when you are winning in life.

13. Delay gratification.

A critical problem among young people is the lack of self-control. When teens view themselves as immortal or invincible, they abandon restraint, caution and common sense—tossing these to the wind. You have a young body, and perhaps good health, and your whole life is ahead of you. It may seem that mistakes made now have nothing to do with your future life. Therefore, it is easy to feel that you should have what you want, now, and do what you want, now. This is not the case. Everything you do *now* makes a permanent imprint on your life. Your attitude, choices, behaviors and experiences, are at this very moment, shaping the adult you are becoming. You take everything with you from your youth into adulthood. When you move into a larger house, you furnish it with your possessions from the old, smaller house. In this same way, you wear the same scars from youth on your adult body.

Often, indulging in excessive, reckless and pre-marital sex is a sign of low self-esteem, emotional wounds or weaknesses. It is reaching for love and is a cry for help. The tragedy is that engaging in sexual activity makes matters worse. If this is your story, seek advice and counseling from a parent or responsible adult. Do not confuse love with lust. Check in with your self to find out what is driving this desire. Pursue other avenues for release, such as sports or hobbies, or harvesting your gift. Find another activity that makes you feel good about your self.

Learning to delay your gratification is critical. This does not mean that you do not enjoy life. It simply means making good judgments. It means involving your self in activities, friends and behaviors that support your growth and betterment. It is choosing self-improvement and forward motion over immediate gratification of physical, sexual or egotistical urges. When you make this choice you may find that you have more youthful fun, security, and freedom and fewer adult worries and fears. You are making a wise investment in your future while enjoying life in the present.

14. Stay in your 'right mind'.

People resort to drugs to escape reality, to enhance pleasure, or to just zone off into an altered state. Drug use of any kind will hurt you. And this includes alcohol. Even when you are experimenting, you are 'choosing' the risk of becoming seduced by this destructive activity. Drug use deteriorates your mental capacity. It keeps you from focusing; it impairs your memory, your thinking, and your ability to speak and communicate—not to mention the damage it does to your body. If your current state of mind or reality doesn't 'cut it' for you, do the right thing! Step into a dream or vision that will give you a *real* high. Choose to stay 'conscious'.

15. Don't be a gloom and doom junkie.

Seventy-five percent of what comes at you is negative! Anger, terror, violence and mayhem are primary ways in which people are entertained. Society glamorizes these. Newspapers, TV, movies, radio and music capture your attention with their pictures of life; however, they are too often messengers of gloom and doom. This bombardment of negative images keeps people feeling fearful and hopeless. It even causes many to feed on other people's pain and suffering in order to feel comfortable and secure.

The villain within thrives on negativity. Understand this. While it may be tempting, and even gratifying, overdosing on such negativity is unhealthy. It prevents you from maintaining the fortitude you need in your journey. Sure it's real. But even here, you can, and must discriminate to control your mental climate.

Your behavior is influenced by your attitude and outlook. And these are often influenced by what you consistently take into your mind. Seek balance. Like your body, respect your mind. Don't put anything into it. Don't overwhelm it with dread. Seek out and expose your self to mental content that celebrate the good things in life. Love, beauty, humanity and goodness can also be entertaining and interesting, when you give them a chance.

16. Take 5!

Being constantly surrounded by family, friends and other people does not necessarily enhance you. It can divert you from doing some of your most important work. And there are other distractions. You have activity-packed days, and there is so much *stuff* going on around you. Your young mind is blasted with 'sound bytes' that come at you hundreds of times a day; data and images are filling up your head, and all too often, with too much garbage. This noisy, split-second information overload also shortens your attention span.

It is cool to be calm. Spending time alone can energize you and get you clear on a lot of things. You can get to know your self better and understand the design of your life. You can learn why things are going a certain way, how your attitudes, beliefs and behaviors may be hurting or helping you. You can come up with answers and solutions to problems. There is so much natural wisdom within you! When you turn down the volume of your life, you are more likely to access your wisdom and be guided by it. You can also hear the soft voice of the champion within.

Learn how to be alone—and enjoy it! Make it a priority and habit to give your self some space to read a book, listen to music, watch a movie, go for a walk, think, reflect or meditate—to recharge your mental and emotional batteries. Constant motion is not necessarily forward motion. You can get a lot done by taking time out to chill.

Meditation
Meditation is making its way into schools and youth programs. Mediation calms and clears your mind. It helps you to focus, stay in control and simplify your life. A few easy ways to do this are: 1. Close your eyes and empty your mind to focus on the moment; and, 2. With your eyes open, practice awareness by noticing your experiences without labeling them as good or bad. This frees and lightens your mind and helps you stay in a good mood.

17. Don't search for problems or drama.
Too much drama and problems drain and distract you. And when you look for and are pre-occupied with these things, they will stalk you. Problems are a part of life. Not to worry, you will have your share of drama, and your 15 minutes of fame. Don't dig for what is wrong; don't run after trouble; and don't feed on other people's tragedy and pain. Search out and see the joy that is already there in your life. The more you look and see it, the more you will have. And that's a fun place to be.

18. Be a leader.
Resist peer pressure at all costs. You may go along with friends, but make sure that you do this because you want to, not because you were pressured. Resist peer pressure even when your friends are well intentioned.

Leaders may be part of a group but they participate because they are self-guided, not because the group pressures them to do so. Whether you go along with the group or not, make sure that the reasons come from you. And make certain that it is a move that will boost, not hinder you. True leaders know that they are the masters of their destinies. They lead themselves in the direction that best supports and sustains their growth.

19. Believe and invest in your magnificence.

You are unique, and you may have some serious talent to unleash. Happiness is maximizing your strengths and exalting your gifts. You have a responsibility to your self to fulfill your potential. There is a stage in the theater of life that belongs exclusively to you. Only you can command that stage. Find that stage, go directly to it, claim it and work it.

Investing your time, energy and resources in your talent increases the likelihood that you can build your career around it. And there is no sweeter success than making money doing what you love!

20. S-T-R-E-T-C-H your self.

Bust out of your routine if you find your self in one. Step outside the vicinity of your neighborhood and circle of friends. Expand your range. Find out about city tours, field trips, or international youth exchange programs. Read books on assorted subjects to grow your perspective and understandings. The more you learn about the world around you, the more you learn about your self. And the more you learn about your self, the less the villain within can sway you.

Stretching your self means taking risks. It is moving beyond your comfort zones. It is to trust your self and to know that life will support you while you do the right thing. As you stretch and get out of the box, you are more creative; you grow your common sense and natural intelligence. The world becomes a different place than it was through the eyes of a naïve person. You see more, and can better appreciate what's out there for you. When you have a larger, richer base of knowledge and possibilities to pool from you are no longer a hostage of the villain within.

21. Put your best face forward!

Whether you are a shy or outgoing person, show the world your best face. Pay attention to how you interact with the people you meet along the way. Unless they prove themselves unworthy, treat them with respect and kindness. Everyone needs these things.

You don't always know what is on the other side of the faces you meet—who they know or what influences they may have. Play your cards right. Learn how to solve problems, how to take and give feedback, and resist conflict. Take people on their face value and try not to stereotype or prejudge. This is not being square or un-cool. It's about investing in your quality of life and success. When you let others see your best face, it reflects back to you. It energizes your life. This sets things in motion for positive things to come your way.

Nothing can be placed into a closed fist. And it takes more facial muscles to make a frown than it does to make a smile. The more you smile at the world, the more things will loosen and open up to you.

22. Pay your dues.

Your career will go through many phases. Every phase prepares you for the next. *For example,* at 16, my first job was working the counter at McDonald's, I also made the shakes and fries! As my career evolved, I became a department store cashier, an office clerk, a secretary, a supervisor, a marketing rep., a business consultant and workshop leader, a university Chair and professor. Some of these jobs I worked while going to school. I am now, the Founder and President of my own company. From each job, I gained skills and abilities that graduated me to the next level.

There is a lot that you must learn along the way while working on your goals. There will be people you *must* answer to, and tests and preparations you *must* undergo.

However, the time will come when you will be well established in your chosen field or vocation. You will no longer be the trainee or apprentice. You will be the expert. Then you will call the shots and will answer to no one, or very few. But much training and learning needs to take place before that time. In fact, you won't get there without this! Do the groundwork necessary to reach your goal. Avoid taking an attitude that you are too good to do something, especially if it offers you a learning opportunity. View all your learning and training as honorable work that supports your evolution as a dynamic person.

Seek out the most promising avenues to hone your skills, not necessarily the best salary. People will gladly pay you to give your all. But do your job so well that not the dead, the living nor the unborn can do it no better.

23. Come to play and play to win!

Let it be known that you came to play and that you played to win, regardless of the outcome. Not everything you do will come up roses or turn into a success or please everyone. What is important is that you do your best. This is what comes through each and every time. Showing up to do your best is life insurance that money can't buy. This is something you can always fall back on, and it guarantees you a good night's sleep.

The way to avoid judging your self negatively, self-abuse, guilt or regrets is to do your best at whatever you attempt, and to *know* it. When you do your best, you can't help but to take positive action. And this makes your life come alive. You can only be the real YOU when you do your best, and it is how you show your self that you love YOU.

24. Grow through your problems.

A problem is a difficult question, matter, situation or person that requires a solution. Problems and challenges are a natural part of everyone's life. You will never be able to avoid them. They help you grow. That is why you have them. And the best you can expect is to get better at solving the problems that are given to you—like doing math. So instead of hoping that they will someday go away, and you will be free of them, you need to apply the tools to deal with them. Often problems and challenges allow you to discover and develop new strengths you will need in your journey.

For example, you may have to juggle many responsibilities as a young person, such as school assignments, extracurricular activities, household chores, and the expectations of parents and friends. And this becomes a problem for you. The situation might be telling you that your life is too busy, that you have filled it with too much activity, and it is difficult to manage. Your challenge might be to develop organizing skills and good judgment. You may have to learn how to set priorities based on what is important to you. You will need these abilities as an adult.

Here are 4 easy steps to meet problems well:

- *Accept them as opportunities to grow.* When a problem arises, reflect and ask your self, *"What is this experience telling me about myself and my life? What is this experience trying to teach me? How can I grow from this experience?"*

- *Pay attention to what is happening to you.* Meeting a problem or challenge well is a direct investment in your growth. Pay attention to what is happening to you in the moment as the problem presents itself. Are you becoming more sensitive, defensive or angry? Are you learning how to deal with fear and to take risks? Are you able to put your self into someone else's shoes? The learning value of the problem has more to do with how you are meeting and experiencing it, rather than the outcome. When you pay attention to what the problem is telling you about your self, you also come closer to finding the solutions.

- *Face it head on—get the lesson.* Don't run away from your problems. Like a pit bull, they will only chase after you, yapping at your heels. Your problems have your name written on them, and will stick to you like glue until you work through them. The same kinds of problems will repeat themselves in your life until you learn how to meet and learn from them.

❖ *Involve others.* Get help and involvement from others if necessary. Some problems may be trying to teach you how to cooperate, collaborate or to trust and receive from others. Let your inner champion guide you on when and how to bring others into the mix.

On self-destruction and teen suicide. Spirit does not present you with a problem or challenge that you do not have the capacity to overcome—given your present skills, ability and resources. The will to self-destruct or to commit suicide are choices. They are the choices to ignore and not pursue the options that are always available to you; to deny your potential; and to destroy a precious life. Ultimately, you let your self down. Because things are always changing, the picture you have today can be entirely different tomorrow. You can always re-arrange things. You can always amend things. When you sink to this point, grab hold of the hands of change.

ᗌᗤᗏ ᗌᗤᗏ ᗌᗤᗏ

There are some situations in life that are tailor-made for you. There are problems that only you must confront and work through in order to stretch and grow. When you face these situations, and with the best resources you have to bear, you come out feeling better— you fear problems and challenges less. From this you may learn something about your self or discover something new about the world around you. But in all cases, the outcome of working through the problem adds value to your life. (See the Spiritual Law of Learning and Growth in Chapter 7)

25. Stay in the light. Burst in with the dawn!
Everyday is a new beginning. Whatever you didn't do well yesterday, you have a brand new chance to get it right today. Don't fade away in the past or shadows. Stay in the light. Let this be a lifestyle! Fear and negative thoughts and emotions are the major causes of teen breakdown. These things, going un-checked and unaddressed

can also lead to teen suicide. As long as you have life and light you have possibilities. You have options.

Staying in the light is all about integrating the tools provided in this chapter, into your daily affairs. Staying in the light means choosing positivity over negativity, choosing truth over lies, and choosing love over fear. Love puts the villain within on lock-down. Staying in the light is letting the energy of love rule in your life. Not because it is a good thing to do, but because it makes good sense. It is love for your self, your talent and your potential. It is love for others, community and love of spirit. The light warms your dreams and brightens the way on your chosen path. It protects you from that which seeks to bring you down, but cannot thrive in the brilliance of its glow.

The truth is the light. So tell the truth. Seek the truth. And hold dearly to what is true about you. Staying in the light is to recognize and embrace the spiritual laws that are active in your life, and conducting your life in harmony with these laws. It is to know that you are a spiritual being having a physical experience, and as an emissary of the light, you are here to shine.

Q & A
A Frequently Asked Question by Teens

"If my parents tell me to do something, is that still my choice?"

Answer: Yes. Even when parents tell you to do something, you make the choice whether to respect and obey them or not. The responsibility of making that choice ultimately lies with you. Your free will to choose is as fundamental and automatic as taking a breath. When you break it down, you will see that you make choices about everything that comes from you.

Chapter Six
Parents' Corner

Parents must get across the idea that "I love you always, but sometimes I do not love your behavior."
—Amy Vanderbuilt

The best way to keep children at home is to make the atmosphere pleasant and let the air out of the tires.
—Jacqueline Kennedy Onassis

Trust yourself. You know more than you think you do.
—Benjamin Spock

There are several factors that shape the adult that your teen is becoming. In priority order, these factors are, parenting, the innate personality disposition in which they were born, culture, socialization and key experiences. The manner in which you parent your child is the single most powerful influence on them, and throughout their lifetime.

In Celebration of Parenting

Parenting is *the work or skill of a parent in raising a child.* As a parent, you are the fountain from which your child's life springs forth. Parenting is a divine responsibility. The fulfillment of this role far outweighs any amount of wealth, fame or fortune.

It would be great if your teen came with a manual. The hardest things in life do not—we simply wing it and find a way. No other post in life requires the kind of work and sacrifices of parenting. Whether you parent as solo, with a partner or spouse, or with the help of family, relatives or friends, it is an enormous task. It is an honorable duty. Through your efforts and capacity you are grooming and presenting a human being to the world. Based on how you set them up, your child will be the source of gladness or sorrow in their own, and in the lives of others.

In the same way that you concoct your best desert or meal to please and impress family and friends, you prepare your child for the world. Your best ingredients of love, nurture, experience, skill and wisdom go into this. With these, your crowning achievement as a parent, can be to launch a human being that:

- Has a positive sense of self.
- Has a sense of decency and a desire to help others.
- Has a sense of direction of where they are going.

If you have achieved this, you have done a great service!

Six pieces of the 'Parenting Pie' will enable you to achieve this.

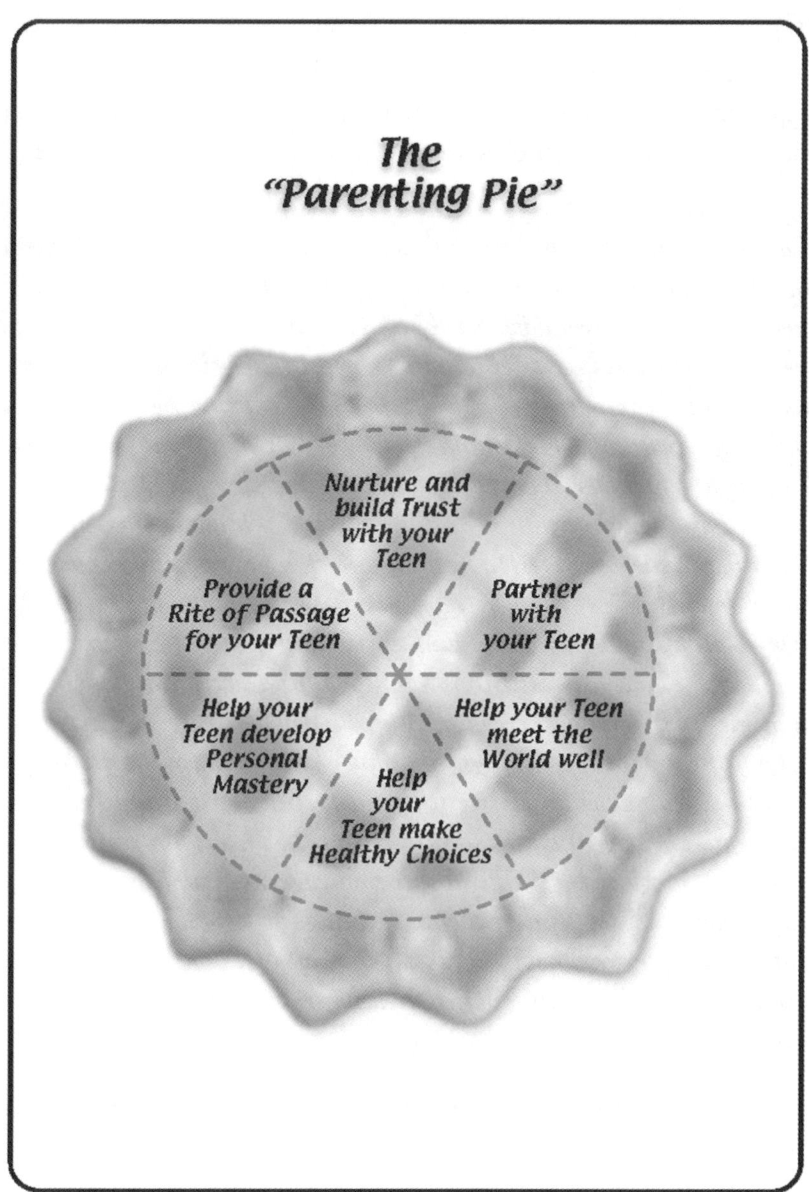

Parenting Pie

Nurturing Your Teen and Building Trust

Teens' emotional and psychological well-being is a direct outcome of parenting. As parents we share an obligation to love and care for our teens, and to nurture their mental health. Nurturing is as essential as food, clothing and shelter. Without it teens don't grow well.

LaTanya's Story

LaTanya is an African-American teen. As far back as she can remember, LaTanya's father repeatedly told her that she was ugly and slow. He was always displeased with her shy and introverted ways. He would tell her that she would never amount to much in life. Her worst memories were of him comparing her to her friends—putting her down while building them up. He would scold her for not being like them. LaTanya remembers being sexually molested at an early age by an uncle. For a long time she kept this to herself because she was afraid to tell other family members. The accumulation of these abuses over time wore down LaTanya's self-esteem. She began to make poor choices in her relationships with boys and men. Her low sense of self drove LaTanya to crave the attention, approval and acceptance of the boys and men who crossed her path. And she was not very selective about whom she sought these things. She gave sex in exchange for a compliment that came too quick, a gift that was cheap or a promise that was not kept. The boys and men she attracted teased her, put her down, and took advantage of her vulnerability and eagerness to please them, and to be loved and accepted by them. At the age of 17, LaTanya was lured into a stranger's car; he told her that she had big, pretty legs and a fine face. He drove her to an isolated area where he beat, raped and abandoned her.

LaTanya, now 19 years old, tells me that the violent rape experience was her "wake-up" call. With counseling and involvement at a community center for 'at-risk' girls, she now sees the pattern of abuse that she slipped into. She recognizes its connection to her low self-esteem, and the choices she made. She understands that the molestation, abuse and rape were wrong. And at the same time, she is taking responsibility to build her self-esteem so that she can make healthy choices in her relationships with men, from now on. She is learning about boundaries, self-respect, and how to love herself as no one else can.

Nurturing your teen is easier and more effective than parents tend to think. And nurturing should begin as early as birth! Here are some things you can do:

1. Love and validate them unconditionally.
Never withhold love from your teen, for any reason. This destroys trust, and fast! When they misbehave, let them know that you love them, but not their behavior. Move from shaming and blaming to validating. Shaming and blaming generates fear and anger in your teen. Create a safe emotional and psychological environment for your teen that they can count on, by accepting who they are, from the top of their head to the tips of their toes—all the time.

Mothers and fathers are the first people to validate the femininity and masculinity of their children; and how this is done sets the tone for teens' future relationships. Tell them that they are smart, pretty, handsome, gifted and unique. Do this in wholesome, appropriate ways.

And please, at all costs, never put them down or compare them to their peers. This is deeply wounding and cripples their development—leaving lasting emotional scars.

2. Respect your teen.
Respect is showing your teen that they have value, that their needs are important. It is treating them in a way that upholds their dignity. This is not to be confused with being weak, a pushover or allowing your teen to control you. When they 'act out', as indeed they will, tell them that you are disappointed or upset; discipline them as you see fit. But do this with regard to their sensitivities and without intruding upon their vulnerabilities. Disrespect breeds more negative reactions than positive ones.

3. Keep your anger in check.
There is bound to be some high-pitched yelling, screaming and hot emotions with a teen in the house. I understand all too well, the itch to go completely "off" on your teenager. But the immediate satisfaction of putting out anger to hurt them may cause you much regret later. If anger is an issue for you, check it. Own it. Do not project your 'stuff' onto your teenager. Don't come at them with anger or rage that has nothing to do with your child. Take a time-out, and get back to them. If the anger is a result of their behavior, let them know that you are angry, but don't beat them over the head with it.

Anger is contagious. It spreads like a disease. When you inflict reckless anger upon your child, they will in turn, inflict that anger upon someone else. I find that my son is more responsive when I tell him that I am disappointed in him rather than to my anger. Model to your teen healthy ways to express anger. Even in your moment of anger you are teaching them.

4. Provide clear boundaries. And be consistent.
Tough love curbs the appetites, impulses and freedoms that don't and won't serve teens well. This includes *attitude!* Issuing clear boundaries helps them to feel safe, loved and cared for, and it paces their growth. Letting teens get away with things is a sign of neglect and abuse. It allows them to venture into territories they may not be able to handle. They do not learn or grow this way. Showing tough love to your teen can be like riding a wild bucking bronco. Because they *will* push back. But have heart. They want and need this from you; and you and your teen will survive this. You are the one to keep your teen tuned in to what is important.

Providing clear boundaries also means helping teens to learn from their mistakes and poor choices. Teach them that poor choices have consequences and that positive choices have their rewards. Teach them that even innocent mistakes have ramifications. Helping them to sharpen their judgment this way is a primal form of parental protection.

It is hard for your teen to trust you when: You waffle and go back and forth on your word; or do not follow through on your promises and disciplines. This also makes it hard for your teen to easily distinguish right from wrong. Be consistent. And if you change up on something make sure that you tell them why.

5. Stay close to them.

Do not assume that you can just turn them loose because they are now, teens. Even though they may act as if they are 'grown', you know they are not. Their lives are still young and tender and they continue to need mothering and fathering from you, but not babying.

6. Be on their side more often than not.

Allow your self to be your child's cheerleader. Check out the facts involving school reports, or other incidents where your child is concerned before coming down on them. Be their strongest advocate when they run up against negative peer pressure or bullying. And when they are wrong, say to them: *"I am here for you. Help me to help you."*

7. Look for their Good.

What parents project onto teens is how teens learn about themselves. Too often, parents are driven to focus on what teens are doing wrong. Too much of this debilitates teens and breaks their confidence and spirit over time. Assume the best about your teen, and find the occasion to praise and encourage them, instead of overly criticizing. Looking for your teen's Good is like taking a glimpse of the part of God that is within everyone. When you validate their Good, it encourages your teen to raise it and to showcase it.

8. Balance negative with positive feedback.

This relates to looking for their Good. When negative feedback is called for, make it a point to include something positive to say, as well. Keep your feedback to your teen balanced. Use what I call the 'feedback sandwich'. This is beginning the feedback with a positive comment; then describing your concerns and observations about their behavior; and ending with some words of encouragement and inspiration. *For example: "I think you have made a lot of progress since last year with your grades. That makes me proud. I am concerned about you not taking initiative to do your share of the household chores. This is not acceptable. What needs to happen for you to take care of your responsibilities here? I understand that you have a lot going on, and I know that you have it within you to do the right thing. Talk to me."* Use your discretion on when this kind of conversation is appropriate.

Use affirming language. When addressing your teen, avoid language that hurts their self-esteem. Do not place labels on them. Frame negative feedback in terms of what they did, not who they are. Teens are not what they do. Instead of saying, *"You are stupid"*, say, *"What you did was stupid"*. Or, *"Your behavior is bad"*, instead of, *"You are bad"*.

9. Discipline, not punish.

To punish is to treat harshly in order to inflict pain and suffering for a wrongdoing. To discipline is to treat in a manner that corrects and develops the self. I understand the impulse to punish with no holds bared, a teen for an offense. But this is a time to take every opportunity to help your teen to grow, and trust you as their partner in growth. Punishment too often defeats this purpose.

Disciplining means giving your teen forewarning of the actions you will take as a consequence of a wrongdoing, especially if your action will be stiff. It means letting them know why you are taking a particular action, because teens cannot always put the pieces together. Harsh punishments and penalties that are not forewarned can produce rebelliousness and alienate your teen from you.

10. Extend the family network.

It remains true that it takes a village to raise a child. This applies even more today. Welcome and surround your teen with responsible adults who may not be family, but have your teen's best interest at heart. Let them share in the joy of rearing a cherished child. There is never too much good love and care for your child to receive. This extended family can also nourish your parent/teen relationship.

11. Rule from love, not fear.

It is more rewarding for your teen to honor and respect you rather than to fear you. Coming at them from fear only teaches them fear, not necessarily fear of you. Teach them love. This means managing your fear, and not using fear as a motivator. It's about role modeling, walking your talk, and summoning the power of love when dealing with your teen. Work from your instincts. You know how to do this. And keep love, not fear, at the center of your interactions with your teen. When communications breakdown, or misunderstandings give rise to tension and distance, keep love present. Tell your teen that, despite what is happening now, you love them.

12. Be mindful of how you exchange energy with your teen.

As humans, we thrive on energy. And more often, families extract energy from one another in negative ways, through pettiness, fussing, neediness, and subtle manipulations. Your teen needs his and her energy to grow. Be aware of this, and steer clear from the unspoken ways that you feed on their life force. Make them aware of this also, because this feeding goes both ways. Seek energy exchanges with your teen that are mutually beneficial.

13. Show your teen affection; lighten up.

Physical affection is a basic human need. Because your teen is no longer a baby or small child, does not mean that they can go without parental affection. The lack of physical affection can cause teens to seek it elsewhere. And that can have dire consequences, such as teen pregnancy or hanging out with the wrong crowd, or worse. Also, too much heavy drama at home with parents drives teens away.

It's OK to show affection. Although teens may shun it, especially boys, trying to be tough, they yearn for some form of loving physical contact. Trust me on this. Pat them on the head, kiss them on the cheek; hug them, hold them; massage their tired shoulders or back;

tickle them. Play with them, for this is a form of affection. Show your silly side, play harmless pranks. I, on occasion have pillow fights and wrestle with my teenage son. And he wins most of the time.

When you lighten up and show respectful physical affection to your teen, you let them know that despite your challenges with each other, that you care about them; and this also helps you to connect and communicate better. You also model to them healthy ways to express love and affection.

14. Nurture their spirit.
Nurturing the spirit that lives inside your teen includes all the above. It is recognizing that they have 'divinity' within them, and are in constant relationship with a Higher Power. According to Reverend Jackie Garner of the *Trinity Center for New Thought*,* the more you reinforce this understanding and model this to them, they will act accordingly. And, parents can and should expect teens to grow into their wisdom. Reverend Garner suggests that one way to do this is to expose and involve them in activities that bring out their creativity and appreciation of beauty.

Nurturing their spirit means telling your teen *that "You are better than that!"* when they exhibit negative behavior.Nurturing your teen's spirit grows it. As their spirit grows they cultivate humility, stay grounded, and are enabled to combat their inner demons.

15. Nurture your self.
You must nurture your self to be able to nurture your teen. Self-nurturing is investing in that which brings you joy. It can be anything you need to do to express your love and care for your self. It could be taking your self out for dinner; treating your self to a gift; taking time out to be alone with your self—to read, watch a movie, or visit with your friends. Nurturing your self also means to show your self some compassion—not being too hard on you, forgiving your self and asking for help when you need it. By nurturing your self you instill this value in your teen—helping them see how this is done.

Partnering with Your Teen

Partnering is a wise and savvy way of parenting today's teen. A partnership between a parent and teenager is a relationship that serves mutual interests. Such a partnership does not diminish the responsibility or authority of the parent. It simply brings parent and teen together in an agreement on how they are going to work together and support one another. I have such a partnership with my teenage son. It is new territory, which I find exhilarating, challenging and rewarding. And it's not perfect.

Every parent and teen may not be able to engage in such a partnership. This has to be weighed in terms of trust levels, styles, and circumstances. But the advantages are something to consider. A partnership: 1.] Positively engages your teen's energy and boosts their self-esteem; 2.] It takes some weight off the parent's shoulders by having a shared level responsibility with their teen; and 3.] It strengthens communications between parent and teen. Ultimately, a parent/teen partnership decreases the chances that your teen will go astray or down the wrong path.

Here are some ways to enter into this kind of partnership:

Personal Growth First!

As you partner with you teen, you are also modeling appropriate behavior and virtues. Therefore, the very first thing that you must do in engaging a partnership with your teen is to commit to a program of personal growth, for your self. Here, you must check in with your self. This means inspecting your communicating skills and personal challenges— what you do well and what you should work on. You must assess how they may show up in this partnership, and commit to owning them. If there are some personal adjustments to be made, then go for it! The important factor here is that you as a parent do not bring your issues or baggage into this partnership. And because we all have these, the least you can do is to own yours when they do come up. Doing this is powerful role modeling for your teen.

Lay Out Your Mutual Goals

Once you have committed to a program of personal growth, work with your teen to lay out the kinds of goals you each want to achieve in this partnership. Keep it simple to a few goals, which might include: Getting A grades in school, parent returning to school, caring for younger family members, making the basketball team, or simply keeping peace in the home.

Steps for the Parent/Teen Partnership

1. **Learn and grow with them.** Let them know that you are still learning and growing, that you are even learning from them.

2. **Move beyond the power and control model.** Although this parenting style may have worked for some of us parents, it falls short on many of today's teens. It may even backfire. Focus on reaching agreements and collaborating. Move from telling and ordering to 'agreements' that hold teens accountable to carry out their part of the deal. And make sure that you follow through on this.

3. **Get to know their friends and teen culture.** Make it a point to know who your teen calls their friends and spends their time. Get to know their friends' parents also. Talk with their friends and join in when they show up. Don't be bullied or intimidated by teen culture or attitudes. Trust in the solid, timeless values that guided you as a teen.

4. **Check in.** Be present with your teen. Turn off your own distractions and give them quality time versus quantity. Show that you are genuinely interested in their world and affairs. Ask them how it's going, and if there is anything they need to discuss with you.

5. **Meet them where they are.** There comes a time when you must simply, 'just flow' with your teen. Meeting them where they are is hanging in there with them during their ups and downs—being in the moment. When they loose or fail or just feel bad, tell them that you understand how hard it is to loose, and that you know how bad that feels. When they are proud and excited, tell them that you are happy with and for them.

6. **Let go.** Understand that your teen ultimately belongs to themselves. You can support, guide and protect, but you cannot control their destiny. This is a hard pill to swallow. But really, it's all good! Teach and release them to unfold as they are meant to. Trust their spirit and the work you've done to get them this far. Loosen and lengthen the leash. Follow closely as they spread their wings and begin their flight of self-discovery.

7. **Be human with them.** Don't be afraid to let down your guard. Let them know that you are human and sometimes afraid. Let them see you make mistakes.

8. **Plan with them.** Set goals and objectives with them that are reasonable, and that match their strengths and limitations. Set up ground rules on how you are going to communicate with each other.

9. **Don't make assumptions.** Refrain from assuming that you know something concerning your teen before checking it out with them. Give them the benefit of a doubt.

10. **Practice bold communications.** Push beyond your comfort zone and fears. Look and SEE what is really going on with your teen, and talk to them about ANYTHING. This makes it more likely that they will come to YOU with their problems and concerns, not someone else.

Helping Your Teen to Meet the World Well

At this stage in their lives, teens need independence to explore and make their way into the world—a world that is very different from the one we as grownups knew as teens. To meet the world well, teens must navigate professional and social relationships, cultural influences, peer pressures, social mores, risk, and rising standards. Life today is demanding and complex for anyone, youth and adults, alike. Today's teen has to practically hit the ground running, especially after high school. They must look ahead and plan their future earlier, and practice greater focus and discipline in order to realize their dreams.

You can help them to navigate their way in the world by preparing them in the following ways:

* *Command their respect.* Children debase themselves when they disrespect their parents. Tell them this. You are the first authority figure they will have to deal with in life. They need to trust and respect the authority figures they will meet in their journey who are there to help them grow. It is better for them to learn to respect authority in a loving home, rather than in an indifferent school or work environment, or from a harsh prison cell. Command their respect, not through fear but through firmness, tough love and walking your talk. You command their respect by keeping the roles between parent and child clear, and by respecting them, and your self.

* *Teach them the concept of paying their own way as an adult.* Help your teen to understand the balance between work and reward. Teach them to appreciate the exchange of work for money and material goods. Give them responsibilities and opportunities to 'earn' what they want, and what they get. Help them to understand that honoring one's debts and the agreements made with others is something that grownups do.

❋ *Discourage violence.* Let them know that violence is its own reward, and only leads to destruction. Teach and show them this by your own example.

❋ *Train them to solve problems early.* The problem-solving part of your teen's brain does not fully develop until ages 21 and 22 on the average. However, they are challenged to meet and solve problems before they reach that age. Give them a head start by encouraging them to figure things out; by listening to their opinions; and by inviting them to help you solve problems.

❋ *Let them know that you've got their back.* It can get overwhelming for your teen as they grow into the world. The many responsibilities, pressures and challenges can be scary. Give them the independence to do as much as they can on their own, while letting them know you are behind them—that you will not let them fall. This kind of back-up helps them with their confidence and strength; it gives them a sense of protection as they learn and grow. It helps them to take the necessary steps, and risks that often come with opportunities.

Parental back-up also means to show up and get involved in their school activities. Partner with their teachers and coaches while avoiding micromanaging; be open, supportive and receptive to the feedback from well-intentioned teachers. Trust your teen's unique way of developing during their journey through school, make your involvement with their teachers objective and free of your own school baggage.

Helping Your Teen to Make Healthy Choices

Everything your teen does will flow from a choice he or she makes. This ranges from deciding what to wear each day, to how they will respond to given situations. Making choices is something teens tend to take for granted. Yet every choice they make impacts some aspect of their life, both in the long and short term. The critical question is, are they going to make healthy choices, and will they take responsibility for the choices they make? Regarding teens' choices, here is the bottom line that parents need to know: *Parental indifference creates the risk of teens making irresponsible choices. And, the measure of love, care and support you give your teen determines the degree of good or bad choices they will make.*

Therefore, your contribution is to create a nurturing environment that inspires your teen to make the best possible choices, and to actively guide them as they make choices. Here are some ways to do this:

- Instill in them the awareness, and fact that they *do* make choices, and are responsible for those choices.

- Do your homework. Provide them with information and the pros and cons of the choices they are making.

- Guide them with your wisdom. And then teach *them* how to do the homework—to research the issue at hand, and weigh the pros and cons before making a choice.

- Teach them to see the consequences of the choices they make. Follow-through on this consistently.

- Teach them that choices made out of anger or high emotions can be faulty or lethal. Guide them to keep a level head and to practice restraint.

Helping Your Teen Develop Personal Mastery

Personal mastery means to actively participant in the creation of one's life, and to keep that life on a high note. It means to stay clear and focused on what is important to you. Personal mastery is a critical discipline that parents can help their teens develop. A teen's life can become bogged down with problems to cope with, and challenges that cause them to lose sight of their goals and veer off their path. There are some practical ways that parents can help their teen become masters of their destiny.

Teens' Personal Mastery

- ✴ Help them 'see' what is possible for them to achieve. Nurture their vision and the gifts they will apply to actualize it. Keep a vigilant eye for what your teen does well, what they do often and what they enjoy doing. This is their 'gift'. Seek not to make them into your own image, but help them evolve as they were naturally meant to. Help them to focus on and appreciate their uniqueness and vigorously support them in developing it.

- ✴ Schedule time with them to assess their strengths and limitations. Help them to bring out what they do well, and to manage and correct the things that can trip them up. List these things, and discuss them openly. Do this in a loving, nonjudgmental way.

- ✴ Direct their energy into hobbies and other productive activities. Remember, anger, restlessness and delinquent behavior are often the results of excess energy that is not being properly channeled.

- ✴ Help them to learn from their mistakes and setbacks, to see challenges as growth experiences. This helps to keep them grounded, and to stick with tried and true forms of coping. This way, they make the most out of what happens to them, the good and the bad.

Providing a Rite of Passage for Your Teen

Rites of passage are increasingly important to instill a foundation of confidence in teens, a sense of belonging and being a part of a greater whole. It also solidifies core values to help them navigate today's world. Giving your teen a 'rite of passage' ceremony as they move into adulthood, is the icing on the cake of good parenting! It frames everything you do to nurture, guide and present your teen to the world!

Gregory's Story

My nephew Gregory was the first teen in our family to have a 'rite of passage' ceremony. At the time he was 19 years old, and not very focused with his life. He had just lost his older twin brothers, Obadiah and Albade, and was in a state of depression and confusion—he was wandering. He had his GED, but had no intention to further his education; and he was working at a job that would lead nowhere. A community of people organized a festive ritual that placed Gregory at the center of our attention, love and support. Relatives, friends and members of the community attended this feast, including educators, a minister and a city mayor. We ate, danced, sang, and celebrated. Gregory made a speech acknowledging that he is now a man; and the Reverend confirmed and blessed him as an adult. The party gathered in a large circle around Gregory, that gently closed in on him, we hugged and prayed over him for a long time. Then we showered him with affirmations, releasing Gregory to the world with our cheers, our energy and our confidence in him. This ritual, along with loving counseling, energized and inspired Gregory to go on to college at Texas Southern University. While there, he led the TSU debate team to win an international championship; he worked as an intern for a major Senator in Washington for two consecutive years; and he graduated with honors as the President of the TSU Student Union. He is now a self-employed businessman, and still reaching for the stars!

A teen gains a lot of energy, power, and momentum when they know that a community is behind them in this way.

What is a 'rite of passage'?

An African oral tradition says that: *"Only through initiation can a life be ordered and well filled."* A 'rite of passage' is a ritual that marks an important stage in a person's life. For teens, it is the initiation into adulthood. Most children never know when they become adults. A 'rite of passage' is the single most important event in their lives that enables them to affirm this.

Rites of passage are goals in motion. It brings the teen as, 'star' into a community experience. The passage is not to be done solo, but is to be celebrated with loved ones, family, friends and other participants. It marks the end and beginning—the passing of childhood, while heralding the onset of adulthood. It is a spiritual escapade with God and what one perceives as the 'Higher Power' at the center.

The average age for a 'rite of passage' is 18—as teens transition out of high school and are legally regarded as adults. In some family traditions a girl's 'rite of passage' is her 'coming out' party at the age of 16. This stage marks teens' development on five levels:

Emotional   Awareness of one's emotions, and feeling things more deeply. Discovering that one's emotions are separate from other people's emotions.

Intellectual   Growing in mental interdependence, and emerging brilliance.

Physical   Experiencing growth spurts, hormone surges and other bodily changes.

Social   Discovering new pressures on how to show up and present oneself to the world. Identity seeking.

Spiritual   Reaching for authentic spiritual awareness and experiences, and freedom from boundaries.

There are several kinds of 'rites of passage', based on culture. Some include: Bar mitzvahs and bat mitzvahs in the Jewish culture; 'vision quests' for Native Americans; or Quinceanera in the Hispanic culture. Debutante balls are held in the general culture for girls, and 'rites of passage' based on African traditions are held in the African-American culture. Resources are readily available to guide you on how to conduct these rituals. They can be found on the internet under 'rites of passage' for teens.

Q & A
Frequently Asked Questions by Parents

"What if my kid still makes bad choices despite the love, care and support I give them? "

<u>Answer:</u> Often, bad choices are made because teens do not see the connection between the choice and its outcome. They cannot always put the pieces together. You must continually remind them that there are always consequences to their choices. Diligently point out to them the outcomes of their choices, both the good ones and the bad, so that they can over time, begin to understand and appreciate this connection. Be actively involved in helping them make good choices, but not overly direct them. It is also important to refrain from shoring them up when they are inconvenienced by their bad choices. The more they feel the 'pinch' of their poor choices, the more they are likely to 'get it'.

"What about the kid who is not decisive and lacks ambition?"

<u>Answer:</u> Make them aware that even being non-decisive and doing nothing is a choice. Help them to see by projecting into the future the fallout of the choice to be indecisive. Remember, you can lead a horse to water but you can't make it drink. Ultimately, you must release them to their destiny, once you are clear that you have done your utmost best.

"What if my kid is not always telling the truth?"

<u>Answer:</u> Raise trust levels by validating them, by speaking to their higher selves, and by avoiding blaming and shaming. You build trust with your teen over time, and by instilling confidence in them that they are safe to be truthful with you.

"What do I do about emotional manipulation from my teenager. My teen pits one parent against the other to get what they want, or withholds affection and attention."

Answer: Manipulation is a learned habit. This unfortunate habit is formed out of fear and a lack of trust and confidence in oneself and others, but mostly within oneself. Name the bad habit, because manipulation thrives when it is ignored and goes unchallenged. Shine the light on this behavior when your teen does it. Don't play into it. Step back, and ask them what are they afraid of, and role model positive ways of getting one's needs met.

⁂ ⁂ ⁂

Teens require attention, intention, time, energy and money. There is no way around this. We as parents must accept and willingly and lovingly welcome the developmental needs of teenagers into our lives. I say this, understanding how demanding and complex life may be for adults in today's world. You have needs and your crosses to bear also. Yet you must resist making teens feel that they are a burden through your attitudes and actions. This will only cause grief for you both. You can, by working as a partner with your teen, let them know about your challenges, feelings and frustrations; and give your self the permission to be vulnerable with them. This is healthy, for it raises their compassion to be supportive of you, and it relieves the pressure for you to try to be all things to everyone.

Raising a teen is a journey in which you, as a parent, can choose to enjoy, stretch and learn something about your self. The man or woman your child becomes may be your finest contribution to the world.

**Trinity Center for New Thought, Mesa Arizona, 480.491.6707*

Chapter Seven

Working with Spiritual Laws

Fearlessness is the first requisite to spirituality.
—Mohandas Gandhi

The price of wisdom is above rubies.
—Job 28.18

Be bold and the mighty forces will come to your aid.
—Goethe

Here is wisdom. There are spiritual laws that are vital to your life. They are often referred to as "the facts of life", or "common sense". These laws are not alien to most people. But it is wise to remind your self of their existence and to live by their simple truths. These laws are there to help everyone reap the love, joy, goodness and abundance that is inherit in the human experience. These laws are perfect, unbiased and absolute. They touch every life, equally, and cooperate with the human will. They are sound, precise and always at labor in your life whether you are aware of them or not. Just as predictably as the sun rises and sets each day, spiritual laws are working with you, all the time.

The tools given to you in this book are based on several spiritual laws. Each law plays a distinct role in your life. However, they are linked and related to one another. Just as you study and observe the laws of mathematics, physics, gravity or nature, you must also observe spiritual laws. Witness and understand how they operate in your own and in other people's lives. Learn to work with them. Learn to live with them. This stuff is real!

The Law of Cause and Effect—*Karma*

There is a basic rule in life: All beings are the rightful owners of their deeds. What you put out, you get back. Every action you take is like a debt you generate. There are good debts and bad ones. Every debt you make will come back to you to be collected. Good deeds will bring good deeds your way; bad deeds bring about bad ones. According to the following proverbs: *What goes around comes around. You will reap what you sow. Treat others as you would have them treat you.* Or, *If you live by the sword, you die by the sword.* These words of wisdom are based on this law of 'cause and effect'. It is also known as Karma. You must always be mindful of what you place into the world, in thought, feeling and deed. Sooner or later, it will come back to you. This is like pouring water into a well that you must drink, someday. You must be responsible of the quality of water you put into that well.

When you give your best to others and to the world, you will receive the best that people and the world have to offer. When you give your worst self to others and the world, you will experience the worst that people and life have to offer. If you steal something from someone today, something will be taken away from you. If you help someone in need today, you will be helped down the line, when you are in need. It's just that simple.

The Law of Attraction

"Thought is a living thing." My grandmother often said this. Put another way: You get what you think about, whether you want it or not. Your thoughts, beliefs and expectations are like powerful magnets that attract situations that match and agree with them. This makes the 'law of attraction' the most potent spiritual law. This law works with you every day, hour, minute, second and microsecond. Like a puppy, anxious to please, wanting you to throw a ball so that it can run to fetch it, this law works similarly with you. It is always there at your beck and call, waiting for you to give it a thought or belief to fulfill. You must be careful with what you throw out. The 'law of attraction' will always make the picture in your mind come true, whether it is a rosy picture or a sad one.

How thoughts work.

A thought is a collection of words in your mind on a given subject. Judgments are thoughts, criticisms are thoughts, reflections are thoughts, opinions are thoughts, assumptions are thoughts, ideas are thoughts. Thoughts come and go, and pass through your mind hundreds of times a day. You bring other people's thoughts into your mind. You exchange them. You give them away. Here are some examples of thoughts:

I knew I would blow it. People are out to get me. I am going to fail. People don't take me very seriously. There is not going to be enough to go around. I must hurry up and get my share. Life is hard. Or, *I am a pretty cool person. This is going to be easy. I can do this.* Thoughts that you entertain over a long period of time become beliefs. Like a sauce that thickens and sticks to a pot, thoughts become a part of your personality. They create your reality. But they are easy to change.

How beliefs work.

Beliefs are thoughts that have become concrete over time. Beliefs are descriptions and deep convictions you have about something. Beliefs are not as easy to change as thoughts. They are fastened to your mind. Your beliefs about your self fall into two categories: 1) You believe you have value and worth and deserve to win in life; or 2) You believe you have no value and no worth and are destined to fail in life.

Beliefs are your private truths about your self, your potential, your heritage and life. Beliefs are silent. But they become so much a part of you that you are hardly aware of them. You take them for granted. They become invisible. But they still have much power. Just as you are unaware of your heartbeat and how your body's systems regulate themselves, you are not aware of how beliefs regulate your behavior and life. What you believe deeply comes true. Like a tape recording, your beliefs are your programmed instructions of how you conduct your life. You always act out the program playing in your mind. And together, your beliefs and actions determine the kinds of experiences you have. If you believe that you are a victim you will act like a victim. When you act like a victim you will be victimized. If you believe that you are stupid, bad, and unworthy of respect you will behave in such a way that people will see you as stupid, bad and unworthy of their respect.

According to the 'law of attraction' you control what you think and believe; and this makes you responsible for most of the things that happen to you—the pleasant and the awful. Parents, friends, teachers, and other people cannot and do not control how you think, feel or behave. You always have control over that. There is no way around this.

The law is very cooperative. It responds to your deepest feelings and desires by helping you achieve whatever you feel you truly deserve—whether it is positive or negative. If you feel hopeless and hate your self, the creative force of this law will provide you with the means to self-destruct. If you truly believe that you have value and deserve to express your talent, these forces will rush to furnish your aspirations.

Therefore, to work favorably and cooperatively with this law you must become intimately acquainted with your thoughts and beliefs regarding your self and your life. If you find that they do not serve you well, change them. Immediately! A movie director who is not satisfied with how a scene is being filmed will say: "Cut, change this script. It's not working here!" You have the same power to smash those hardened and self-defeating beliefs and write a new story.

The Law of Change

Things change. The one thing you can really rely on in this life is change. Change is the only constant. Got it? Ok, here we go. This law is the one that really knocks people off balance the most. It seems to go against the grain of how people want to live and work. Many people just don't get it, and spend their lives resisting the inevitable tides of change—like Don Quixote fighting windmills. When you get it, you are really on to something.

Life is dynamic. The young turn old. Seasons come and go. Technology mutates. People transition and transform. Change is necessary for growth. Without it, progress is impossible. It seems as if once you become settled and comfortable in a situation something happens to upset the flow. At first an unexpected change can be upsetting and threatening. It pressures you to do something that takes you out of your comfort zone. But eventually, when you choose to embrace the change, you find your self taking on a new way of doing things that is often an improvement over the old way. That is the beauty of change. It gives you an opportunity to grow and improve the quality of your life—if you allow it to do so. *For example,* a person may have been working at a particular job for many years and all of a sudden that person gets laid off. That person can take the change as an opportunity to grow; or they can choose to resist the change by clinging to blame and wanting the old way back.

When looked at positively the change gives that laid-off person the chance to learn new skills that may land them a better job. That new job might pay more money, and be a job that they enjoy and perform much better. It may be a job that allows that person to discover and bring out a new skill or talent.

Change is like the wind that blows through the trees, pulling the dead leaves off the limbs and making space for new ones to grow. The tree grows stronger by having new, healthy leaves that better absorb the sunlight.

When life sees that you are not growing it will bring about a change to bust you out of your routine. It will present you with a trial to make you participate more fully in life and to honor your gifts and potential. Change shakes things up and forces you to react. When you think about it, you are always reacting to some kind of change. Bucking change intensifies the problems and challenges you may have, and then you suffer; like struggling against the currents of a river. Learn to accept change and flow with it. Make it your friend. Be flexible and adaptable. Trust change. Expect it.

The Law of Learning and Growth

The imperative to grow is inherent in all life forms. Life is a journey where lessons must be learned along the way. Everyone is here to evolve and progress. And it is more important to pay attention to the lessons you are learning in the present, than to live too much in the future. You will learn some lessons while kicking and screaming, and others through the tears of joy. When you are not learning and growing you fall into the ranks of the walking dead.

When you look back on your life 5, 10 and 50 years from now, you want to be able to see how you have progressed and evolved. This occurs in five ways: Emotionally, mentally, socially, physically and spiritually. Accumulating money and material goods is not necessarily learning and growing. These things decorate your life. When you reflect on your journey, you want to see if you have become smarter, more loving, more giving or wiser. You want to see if you have sharpened your talent; or graduated from one level to the next in your career. You want to see how many lives you've touched, and if you put something useful into the world.

You are always exactly where you are supposed to be. There may be many things going on in your life that frustrate you and that you cannot control, such as the behavior of family members, teachers, employers, friends, prejudice and social institutions. There may seem to be more problems and challenges in front of you than fun, peace and calm. Perhaps, someone else's life may even be more appealing to you than your own. The truth is that no matter who you are, who your parents are, or where you live or go to school, you are exactly where you are supposed to be. The problems and challenges presented to you are tailor made for you. You are in that situation to learn something that you need.

For example, dealing with a teacher who you feel does not like you may be a test for you to overcome your sensitivity. You may be more sensitive than others and easily take things personally when they are not. You may feel that you are being singled out or picked on. This may be an opportunity for you to learn how to assert and express your self to an authority figure; and to negotiate with that teacher her expectations and your learning needs. And because everyone is here to learn, that teacher will learn something about her communication skills by you approaching her. From you, she may learn how to adjust her teaching style to accommodate different modes of learning.

Growing up in the 'inner city' of Chicago taught me some valuable lessons. I learned a lot about human nature, and about good and evil. I came out of that experience appreciating things that most people take for granted. I know what it is like to go without food, shelter, clothing, safety and affection. Although my family was poor and struggled, I learned how to laugh from the madcap antics of my three brothers; and I learned how to be organized, efficient and disciplined from my mother. Today, I can better appreciate having my needs met, and I cherish the power of laughter. The skills, knowledge and wisdom I acquired in my early life helped me to triumph over life-threatening problems and obstacles as an adult. I may not have been able to learn what was necessary for me to know from any other kind of upbringing. For that, I honor my roots. And yes, I am still learning.

Your lifestyle may have hurdles and lessons for you that are similar to mine, and perhaps they may be very different. But in any case, you are living the life that is meant for you, because it is the only life that will teach you what you need to learn in order to grow in the way you are destined. And remember, you are learning so that you can develop your uniqueness and give it to the world. There is always support in the world for you to grow in whatever direction you choose.

The key to learning and growing is to understand and appreciate the growth lessons that your life holds for you. No particular lifestyle has value over another. They are all equal! Rich or poor, black or white, the only inequality is how people grow their spirit. And you grow your spirit by meeting your challenges well, and learning and growing from them. Lifestyles are like shoes. You cannot wear a new pair of shoes until you have walked around in and outgrown the old ones. Likewise, you must weather the challenges and learn the lessons from your current experience before growing out of it and into another lifestyle, perhaps a more desirable one. Do not place a low value on the lifestyle you have. Avoid putting it down, or trying to escape from it. Instead, learn from it. When you get the lesson that it is trying to teach you, you are free to move on.

This spiritual law dictates that when you are learning and growing you are happier and life is more interesting. You vibrate at a higher level and are magnetic—attracting the things that you want and that keep you moving forward.

The Law of Choice

Again. You always choose how you are going to think, feel and behave. The primary ability and power you have in life is your will to make choices. When you think about it, everything you thought, felt or did within the past 24 hours came from a choice that you made. This realization can be either liberating or a burden. In either case, the truth is clear, you are never presented with a situation where you cannot or do not choose how to respond. Deep huh? This is a spiritual law that is firmly fixed in your life as a teen and emerging adult.

A person chooses to feel angry when someone insults him or her. No one makes that person angry. A person chooses to cop an attitude, cut a class, join a gang, hit somebody, do drugs, read a book, meditate, or share a story. All these things are choices people make.

The beauty of life is that you have so many choices to make. They are unlimited. And they belong to you, alone. What immense power you have over your life!

So with this power you can choose to like your self. You can choose to see your life as a joyful unfolding. You can choose to see the many avenues for you to grow and meet the world well. You can choose to see your life as a brilliant picture that you paint with the bright colors of your positive thoughts, beliefs and choices. You can choose to believe in your potential to achieve whatever you set your mind to. Regardless of what anyone says, thinks, or does, you are *never* without your power to choose. Choose to use this power responsibly.

The Law of Guidance

When you sincerely seek to grow and achieve something, you will always have natural guidance to help you. The earnest seeker is never alone. Guidance comes to you in many forms. It can be a creative insight or inspiration that pops up in your head. It can be a strong urge to go in a given direction—to read a certain book, to take a specific course, or to just, show up somewhere. Guidance also comes through people who may come into your life to support you. Guidance can come from a stranger who, in passing, gives you a message that you needed to have at that time. Doors to opportunity and resources open where you may not expect them.

The 'law of guidance' always gives you what you need and when you need it, to become a better person and to enhance your life.

What it gives you may not be what you wanted, but it will be what you need. This law is always 'right on time'.

To work with this law you must first have an earnest desire to be creative and constructive. Second, you must apply the talent and resources you have in the present moment. Third, you must ask for guidance and trust that your quest will be supported, and that your needs will be met. Finally, be open, aware, and ready to receive guidance when it comes. And when it does, say *Thank you,* because this keeps the law on your side.

The Law of Abundance

Life is rich and generous. Good things are always 'en route' to you. You were meant to have what you want in this experience, and spiritual law is set up to make that happen. The 'law of abundance' is there to fill the orders you place through your thoughts, beliefs and expectations, ten times over! It is eager to release to you all that is your birthright, which are joy, love, opportunity, achievement and success, regardless of your circumstances. Just as there are infinite stars in the universe, there are untold possibilities awaiting you. Life wants to give you much, because that is how it is supposed to be! There is more than enough of what is good for you, to go around.

The 'law of abundance' meets you where you are. It builds on what you already have and what you are already doing, and it is triggered by your strong desires. To activate this law you must tear down the wall of limiting beliefs that block life's gifts for you; and clarify your expectations. It is to appreciate and work with what you have in the moment. And it is to open up, expect and be ready for abundance—to trust that life is splendid, and that you can have your fair share of 'all that is good'.

Do not think that someday when you are grown up things will miraculously fall into place. There is nothing magical about being an adult that makes things work themselves out, or come to you. Don't wait or procrastinate. The seed work must begin with what you have now, as a young person. If you are an artist, then draw, and draw now. If you are a singer, then sing, and sing now. If you see your self becoming a scientist, then study science courses, now. Do what you can do *now* to give rise to your vision.

The Law of Gratitude

One of the most important things you can say is "Thank you." These two simple words, said with sincerity and regularity have immense power!

The 'law of gratitude' requires that you refrain from taking things for granted, both your blessings and your tribulations. Saying 'Thank you' in your private mind for your many blessings magnifies them. Saying 'Thank you' for the tests that are teaching you helps you to work through them. The 'law of gratitude' multiplies your fortunes, two, three, and ten times over when you say 'Thank you', with a full heart. This attitude of gratitude is the key that opens the door to abundance.

Gratitude enhances your well-being, and keeps a positive flow of energy in your affairs. When you are thankful and appreciative, it is hard for negativity to penetrate your zone. Gratitude shields you from worry, despair and hopelessness. And it also fosters good health.

Work with this law! It's easy. Take some time each day to genuinely appreciate what you have that makes you joyful. And there is always something to be grateful for. You can say "Thank you" for anything. A soft breeze on your face; a baby's smile; a kind word or a gift, are things to be thankful for. A lesson learned the hard way, and the beginnings of peace are things to be thankful for. You can say, "Thank you" after completing a difficult task or assignment, or for waking up refreshed in the morning. The occasions for gratitude are all around you.

The Law of Love

You go a lot farther with a little bit of honey. When you laugh the world laughs with you. And, *Everybody loves a lover.* These are the common lore about the power of love. And they speak to a deeper truth, as well. They are based on the 'law of love'. Love, compassion and kindness are the fuel of a good life. People are responsive to a smiling and a loving nature, because love brings about peace and joy in the world. In this sense, positive social change indeed, begins with one person, YOU.

<u>*Love is.*</u> Love is pure, positive, raised energy. Love is a basic human need. It is as essential as food, air, water and rest. Few people, if any, can survive without it. That is why love is always welcome and generates a favorable reaction from most people. When your attitude radiates from a core of love you will experience a more satisfying life. You give and receive love in the forms of help, kindness, compassion, generosity, companionship, support, affection, forgiveness, nurturing, understanding, and acceptance. Tough love is holding others accountable for their choices and actions. Loving others by holding them to a higher standard encourages them to bring out their best.

Being loving does not make you weak. That is a huge misunderstanding. To the contrary, love is strength. When you radiate love it is difficult for people to manipulate you with fear and anger. Love raises the level of positivity, possibility and light in your experiences, and takes your life to a higher vibration. This gets back to the 'law of cause and effect': Love returns to itself.

On the other hand, resentment, cynicism, guilt, anger, shame and hate are the products of fear. The lack of love drives people to indulge in these vices. These things poison your life. They produce problems, tragedy, and can even make you ill. They are the major causes of human conflict, pain and failure. These things attract counter forces into your life. They close doors where love opens them. They bring you people who will abuse you, where love attracts

116

support and protection. They make you lazy and self-destructive, where love energizes you and inspires you to dream. These negativities are like a heavy weight that pulls you against the flow of the smooth currents of life.

There is plenty love to go around, enough for you to give and enough for you to receive. You control the quality of your life by allowing love or hate to come from and to you. As a young person who has your life ahead, you, most of all, must learn how to manage love and fear. Maintain a loving attitude towards your self, and others, and fill your life with people who share this vibe with you.

The Law of Self

All that exists has a reason. This is because all that is in life is connected. Everything has a purpose to fulfill, from the tiniest insect to the most massive creature. Everything plays a part to make this planet a place where the spirit of life can flourish. Insects help to cultivate the soil for agriculture, flowers surrender their visual and fragrant delights, a sunrise inspires and raises hope, a puppy comforts and amuses. Every person has a role to play in the greater scheme of things. As a human being, you have something unique to contribute to this tapestry of life. This is the 'law of self'.

The world needs your light. You are here to shine. If you have not claimed your unique potential, it is waiting to be unearthed. It is waiting for you to give it to the world. That is why you have it! No one can contribute in the rare way that YOU can. No one! What you give to the world will make it that much better. What you do not give will make it that much worse. You are the one to give your song, your verse, your technical or scientific know-how, your dance, your art, your product, your service, your smile, your wisdom and love.

You discover your gifts by getting to know your self, and by taking the time to listen to your heart. What does it tell you? What is your bliss? Get to know what you enjoy doing, what you do well, and what makes you come alive. Once you discover your bliss, you can make the noble choice to apply your self positively to develop it. You must trust your talent, your self and the 'law' to stretch and take risks. Pursue goals that are interesting and keep you occupied, but are not overtaxing. Be patient, stick to these, give them time to blossom. When you make the choice to develop your talent and apply it in the world, remember that the 'law of self' will not require anything of you that is not already within you to give.

The Law of Connection

Everything is connected. There is a natural kinship among the elements in life, whether it is people, actions or experiences. All things in life are here to nourish and support everything else in this great arena. One person's suffering or joy affects everyone in the world, on some level. People share this planet to learn and grow through one another.

The 'law of connection' calls upon you to be a 'member of the world at large'. It requires you to meet and greet every person on your journey with your best self—to bring your "A" game to every stage and scene. This is because you do not know where your contacts with people or your experiences will lead.

Your personal development is ALWAYS linked to the people who cross your path. You need connections in order to reach your goals. You cannot reach them without other people. The steps you take and the associations you make along the way are like pieces of a puzzle being put into place. You cannot see the entire puzzle. You experience it as just a piece at a time. But as you progress on your path, making healthy choices and doing the things that you know you should do, the pieces fall into place. You see the mysteries unravel, on by one.

Your relationship with the world is just as important as your relationship to your self. The more you open up, expand your horizons and appreciate the connections that are all around, the more possibilities and opportunities will come your way. The more you connect your goals to a larger purpose, the more meaning you will have in your life, and the richer this experience will become for you.

The Law of Service

The 'law of service' is about serving a higher cause and the common welfare through your good works. The 'law of service' requires people to recognize and honor the connections among them, not simply take up space on the planet. Although the choice to be of service to a cause outside your self is an option, you are still bound to this law. You are not in harmony with this law when you center your life around your needs, alone. Because we are all bonded at some level, we are truly our brother's keeper.

By way of your learning and growth, you make a positive impression in the world and touch other lives. The more you contribute to the well-being of others and life on the planet, the more you raise your own life.

The 'law of service' requires that you pursue goals that not only benefit you, but the human community. This could pertain to world health, environmentalism, social issues, government, business, entertainment, medicine, healing, or volunteer work.

This does not mean that you set out to change the world. No one can do this. And you will wear your self out from trying. Fear has a mighty grip in the world, which is in need of so much healing. This is what calls many people into service. Fear is the real enemy, which is the father of anger, hate, ignorance, small-mindedness and negativity, all of which leads to pain and suffering. On the average, 5 out of 100 people will be helped to escape from the grip of fear. As you step into service, know this.

However, the 5% of people you help will in turn, help another 5%, and that 5% will help another 5% and so on. So you can touch many lives. As for the remaining 95%, wish them growth and show them compassion, for this is also a form of service.

Service is about being detached from the outcomes of your good deeds. It is not about bragging or bringing attention to your self, nor seeking praise from others. To do this goes against the law. When this is done, it is not about service; it is about serving ego. And remember, ego is "_E_dging _G_od _O_ut".

When you set out to be of service, remember you should enable others, not do their healing work for them. Help them to help themselves where this is possible. As the saying goes: It is better to teach someone how to fish than to give them the fish.

And ultimately, understand that service is not sacrifice. Take care of your self so that you can be able to help others.

Conclusion
Fade Out

Your life is your most precious possession. You live in a world ringing with possibilities, wonder and support for you. You have the tools you need at your fingertips right now, to begin making your life whatever you want it to be. Your biggest obstacles are not your parents, your upbringing, the system, lack of money, your race nor childhood wounds. Your biggest roadblocks are the kinds of thoughts, beliefs and feelings you entertain and the choices you make.

Your personal growth begins first, with your choice to take control of your life. Second, apply the tools provided in this book that are designed to help you get your life moving. And finally, let your self be guided and supported, always, by the spiritual laws I have shared with you. Let them be your guiding lights and your truest friends.

All the best to you!

What You Can Do—
A Quick Reference

This reference gives you quick access to the numerous life tools and navigational skills provided in this book. You can reference those areas that most concern you at any given time. These areas include family and relationships (Chapter 3), navigational skills to meet the world (Chapter 4), and tools on how to manage your inner life (Chapter 5). Just select the area of need, then choose the wisdom that applies to you right now, and go directly to it.

Chapter 3
Family and Relationships

Here are life tools on how to be strong for your self whether your family is supportive or non-supportive.

Chapter 4
Steppin' Out—Navigating Your Way in the Real World

Here are key navigational skills to help you overcome obstacles and maximize your opportunities.

Chapter 5
Straight Up! Taking Charge of Your Life

Here are life tools that help you manage your inner world of thoughts, beliefs, feelings and choices.

A Step-by-Step Guide to Setting Goals

A goal is an object or a result that you want to attain. You can have a single or several goals at a time. Setting goals enables you to make the leap from what is possible to what is real. When you set goals, the sky is the limit. Choose any direction you want to go, as long as it is forward. You will have many goals throughout your journey. And a noble goal to stick with is to ***exalt your gifts***. Build your other goals around this core one.

Get your vision together. A goal begins with a vision. The vision sets the stage for the goal that you want to achieve. You must 'see' your self acquiring, doing or experiencing something before you can achieve it. It must be something you can achieve through your gifts, skills and resources. Speak this vision out; draw it; write it down. Keep a symbol of this vision close to you.

Put together your cheerleaders. These are the people with whom you surround your self that will help you stay on track and support you. They are your *vision builders*. Include people in your circle of cheerleaders who also have a vision. This circle of people may change as you grow and become older, and as your goals change. But there should always be *vision builders* within your circle as you reach for higher goals. The *vision blockers* are only there to tell you what you can't do and generate interference to your flow. They should not enter your circle. Remember, some people have eyes but no vision.

Step One

Set little goals to build successes into your life. In the beginning, give your self little goals that you can easily reach—goals that do not make strong demands on your time and energy but are satisfying to pursue. These initial goals should allow you to experiment and succeed at whatever you are attempting at the time. Be easy on your self. *For example,* your goal may be to make the varsity basketball team, or to raise your grades from "C" to "A" average. Reaching these easy goals will make you feel like a winner. They will help you discover your talent, ability and bliss. They will boost your confidence to think big and set larger goals.

Step Two

Visualize larger goals. Be specific and think global. Create a picture in your mind of what your future looks like. Decide what you want to achieve and who you wish to become. What do you see? Focus on the clearest picture possible, putting in as much detail as you can. *For example,* what kind of work do you see your self doing? Where does it lead you? What kinds of people surround you? How do they treat you? Where do you live? What kind of clothes do you wear? What is your social status? See it and write it down.

Set your sights high. Think out-of-the-box. Don't limit your self or believe you cannot achieve something until you have reached for it. Try something new. The world is in great need of new ideas and ways of doing things. It has many problems to solve. People need to evolve beyond fear and negativity. There is a lot of work to do. You have the potential to help make the world a better place. It needs more artists, scientists, environmentalists, humanitarians, engineers, thinkers and healers. Chart your purposeful course. Seek the road less traveled. Avoid the crowds. Go for it!

Visualizing is to:

❖ Find out what you enjoy doing.

- Decide if your goal is something you can, or already do well.

- Make sure that it is realistic and you can see YOU achieving it.

- Determine why you want to pursue this goal. Is it for money, fame, material need, to prove your self, to help others or something else? Be very clear about why you want to pursue a particular goal.

Step Three

Develop an action plan. Read and talk to people; do your homework. Identify specific steps that you will take to achieve your goal. You will know this based on your research. *For example,* do you have to go to college? Do you need a certain amount of money? Do you need to learn a new skill or a new language? Do you need a mentor in the field of your choice? Do you need a certain kind of internship or apprenticeship to prepare your self? Will you have to adopt new habits or make new associations? Who do you need to call? Who do you need to know?

Put together a time frame or schedule. When do you want to attain this goal? Work with a daily plan.

Step Four

Execute your plan. Get moving. An idea is just a wish, without the energy and action to give it momentum and reality. Once you determine what steps to take, just do it. You take one step forward and the creative forces that are always there to support your efforts will take two steps towards you. This is a spiritual law of 'learning and growth'. A house gets built one brick at a time. Taking each, required step in your action plan will accelerate you to your goal.

Step Five

Identify resources and support. Identify the resources available to you for support. There are school and community programs for youths; there are corporate internships and job preparation initiatives; and there are nationwide projects that offer a variety of support services and learning experiences. You can learn about them through your school counselor. Determine what you need in order to develop your talents and abilities.

Remember, your cheerleaders are an important part of your resources. Tell people what you want and where you are going. Let them help you. And also remember that when you have a powerful dream you will naturally invite opposition from others. There are people who will feed pigeons yet shoot at eagles. Do not let anyone 'check' you because you have a dream. Choose wisely. The cheerleaders on your team will defend your dream and fly high with you.

Step Six

Persevere, be persistent and keep the faith. Don't give up when things get tough. Understand that you will naturally run into roadblocks along the way. Don't be discouraged by them. Find a way to go over or around those bumps in the road. Overcoming roadblocks will make you stronger, and make the achievement of your goal sweeter.

Never lose faith in your self, nor in the support and humanity of others. Do not lose your confidence in the creative forces that are always there for you. Believe in the goodness of people and that they want to help you. Believe that you deserve to attain your goals. Believe in your gifts. Believe in possibilities.

A Step-by-Step Guide to Building High Self-Esteem

Next to your life, your self-esteem is your most precious possession. Your self-esteem is a measurement of your personal worth. That measurement is whatever you want it to be. You can see YOU as a 'zero', or worth millions of dollars, or even priceless. You can see YOU as being worthy of respect and success and not. Your self-esteem is the way you feel about your self and what you believe is possible for you. It is the range you set upon your horizons. This basic belief determines what you will experience throughout your life.

You control your self-esteem. Your self-esteem is like the engine of a car. It requires proper maintenance and care. A car will not run well on a poorly maintained engine. Likewise, your life will not run well if your self-esteem is poorly maintained—if the value you place on your self is low.

You control both high and low self-esteem. You are already doing it—at this moment. The good news is that you can raise your self-esteem to a higher octave.

The power of positive thinking is at your fingertips. To keep your self-esteem high you must get into the habit of feeding your mind wholesome thoughts and beliefs. Like healthy food nourishes the body, positive thoughts and beliefs nourish your self-esteem. Over time, the body that was fed healthy food shows vigor and vitality, while the body that was fed junk and unhealthy food shows illness, weakness and decay. Your self-esteem works in this same way.

People wear their self-esteem. You can usually tell if someone has positive or poor self-esteem by looking into his or her face and eyes. Positive people tend to look lively, they seem to be on a merry mission, and you feel good around them. Negative people tend to cast a shadow. They tend to be troublesome and pre-occupied with problems and worries. They exude a lack of confidence, and they are doubtful. They drain and bring you down. You can also determine a person's self-esteem by observing the quality of their experiences.

You can believe your self out of anything. These days it takes effort to keep self-esteem high, because you constantly have negative messages, criticisms, images and impressions thrown at you. But once you are in the habit of being positive about your self, your potential, and life in general, it becomes easy. It becomes second nature. You can choose which beliefs you will accept and which you will reject. It becomes as easy as sorting through a box of toys—discarding those toys that are damaged and broken, and keeping those that are intact and in good working condition.

When sorting through your box of beliefs, reject cynicism and feelings of worthlessness. Reject being a victim. Select beliefs that say good things about you—that you are worthwhile, special, talented, pretty, handsome, loving, likable, smart, in command and in demand. Polish up these beliefs and preserve, protect and display them. With practice you will become a pro at sifting through your box of beliefs.

Now that you know that you have control, here are four steps to build and maintain high self-esteem.

Step One

Replace those old mental tapes with new ones. Everyone plays a mental tape in the mind. Many people take for granted the things they say to themselves on these tapes. Mental tapes are like the music that is burned onto a CD, or the data on a computer disc. However, the information you hear on your mental tapes are your own thoughts and beliefs about your self, your potential and place in life. They can be very helpful or utterly destructive to you. Your thoughts and beliefs were programmed into your mind during your childhood experiences, and by the messages that you absorbed over a long period of time. The thoughts and beliefs programmed onto your tapes come from the media, television, friends, family teachers, counselors and so on.

As a child you could not think for your self, and you took on other people's thoughts about you —namely, parents and relatives. These thoughts shaped the beliefs that you hold about your self today. These beliefs were reinforced by society and your experiences growing up. Your parents and other people programmed you to feel either worthwhile or unworthy—to love your self or to hate your self. They did this by putting you down—calling or treating you as if you were stupid or ugly, or by doing the opposite—giving you praise, and building you up because they felt that you were special. They did this by either taking care of your needs or neglecting them. Your parents had a lot of power then, to shape the beliefs you have about your self today. But how they shaped you does not have to be permanent. You have that same power now, as an independently thinking and feeling person, and as a self-guided individual.

What thoughts and beliefs are you playing on your tape? Whose voices do you hear? What do they tell you? Are these voices now becoming your own? Many of you were programmed to view your self and your place in life negatively. Here are some examples: *"I'll never be able to do that. I'm not that good. I wish I could be as talented as her. People don't like me because I'm this or that. I'm too fat. They don't care what I have to say."* And this internal dialogue goes on and on like that.

You cannot truly honor your self unless you clear the negative beliefs and programming from your mind. You must delete these tapes!

Pay attention to the thoughts and beliefs that you are playing on your mental tapes. What you say over and over again in your mind about your self comes true. In the same way you can erase and re-record images on a video cassette, or delete and re-program information onto a computer disc, you can erase, delete and re-program negative beliefs about your self.

But you must first get in touch with what you are playing on those mental tapes.

When you hear negative thoughts and beliefs playing in your mind, catch them! And immediately replace them with new ones that say just the opposite. *For example,* when you catch your self saying, *"I will never be able to do that,"* say to your self *"That is not true. I am in the process of learning how to do that."* The more you catch those negative beliefs and replace them with new positive ones, the fainter the old program will become. This requires paying attention, discipline, and a commitment to your self. Take your self seriously. And be patient with your self because those old tapes were not programmed overnight.

Step Two

Learn to criticize your behavior, not your self. This may sound a bit tricky. But there is a big difference between criticizing what you do and who you are. And this is an important difference. When you criticize your self you are putting your self down and negatively labeling your self. You must always try to give your self the most positive and loving feedback possible. Give your self the benefit of a doubt. There will always be people, practically lining up, to criticize and put you down. Period. When you criticize your self, you are defeating your own purposes. You are turning up the volume on the negative tapes that are already playing in your mind. You are placing damaged and broken toys into your treasure box.

It is easier to change your behavior than it is to change YOU. Criticism is naturally unpleasant and even hurtful. Most people don't respond well to it. Criticizing only your behavior protects you, from your own criticism. Here, you are not punishing your self with negative words that you probably don't need. It is *what* you did that was questionable or wrong, not *who* you are. When you criticize only your behavior, you are free to decide how you want to behave from that point on—which might be differently. You are not burdened with shame and feeling inadequate. *For example,* avoid saying *"I am so stupid."* Instead say, *"I did a stupid thing."* Or *"That was a stupid thing to do."* Here is another example. Instead of saying *"I am so fat."* Say, *"I could lose a little weight."* Or you could say, *"I have a unique figure that works for me."* Learn how to do this when you feel tempted to criticize other people, as well. And if you must go there, criticize their behavior, *not* who they are. As you practice on other people you get better at doing this for your self.

Also watch how much you apologize for your self. Over-apologizing for your self is a clear sign that you have some negative programming that needs to be cured.

Step Three

Stick to your positive beliefs. Once you have gotten into the habit of programming positive thoughts and beliefs onto your mental tapes, stick to them. Guard and hold on to them, because they are precious. Do this in good times and when you are being heavily challenged. The greater the adversity or challenge you face, the tighter you need to cling to these positive beliefs. They are your lifeline. Don't let anyone make you doubt these. Don't let anyone talk you out of them. The more firmly you hold on to positive beliefs about your self, the more they will change your life for the better.

Step Four

Put together a tight support team. As you decide to install a fresh positive program onto your mental tapes, surround your self with people who will support these new beliefs. You are creating a precious circle of life that celebrates who you are. This is your sacred space, be selective about who enters it. Choose to allow and bring people in that are winners, not losers. Your criteria for them to be a part of your sacred circle of life should be the following:

1. They care for and about you.

2. They share your values and key interests.

3. They support your growth and development.

4. They are progressive-minded and have goals.

5. They reinforce and validate the positive beliefs you have about your self.

A bad support team can break your life down. These criteria make it easy to distinguish between your real support and those who mean you no good.

Step Five

Forgive those who put those old negative tapes into your mind. The people who put that negative programming into your mind need your understanding, compassion and forgiveness. Whether they were parents, relatives, teachers or others, they were working with the wherewithal they had at the time. What they said and felt about you was really how they felt about themselves. It had nothing to do with who you *really* are and who you are becoming. Forgive them.

Forgiving them will free you from the tyranny of the past. It frees you from the power that negativity had over you. It frees you to now and forever, define your self. And as you forgive them, you must still protect the healing work you are doing on your self. This means staying clear of abusive and counterproductive relationships that only bring you down. Love those who injured you from a distance as you move on down the road into freedom, joy and light.

Some Basics on Managing Conflict

A New Attitude About Conflict

Conflict plays a major part in any relationship, whether it involves differences of opinion, opposing agendas, the clash of personality styles or ways of communicating. The potential for conflict is always there as you engage the world of people. And managing conflict is a skill that you will need. First of all, begin to adopt a new attitude about conflict, whether you are enbroiled in one or not. Don't be afraid of conflict. It is a necessary part of growth. See conflict as an opportunity to learn about your self and the other person. Here are some basic steps:

1. *Choose to back off.* This is not a time for false pride. Some things you just have to let go. Pride is indulging an inferior situation out of ego, whereas dignity is rising above it. Choose to act with dignity. You can always take time out in the moment of conflict by saying *"I'll get back to you on this."* Come back later when you have cooled off and leveled your mind. Weigh the outcomes of any action that involves emotions. Never allow your ability to choose wisely become compromised.

2. *Pick and choose your fights carefully.* You don't have to jump into every conflict that turns up. Discern whom you are dealing with in the conflict. Is the person emotionally stable or prone to violence, backlash or other forms of aggression? Are they looking for a fight? Also discern if this conflict is about you or not. Are you being pulled into someone else's drama? Is it worth it? Is it likely to come to a reasonable, peaceful outcome? Make a responsible choice here.

3. ***Don't bring anger into the conflict.*** Avoid attacking the other person, either verbally or physically. It will only intensify the conflict and escalate the negativity. Keep a level head, work with the facts and leave your emotions out of it.

4. When you choose to engage the conflict, ***LISTEN.*** Don't hog up the space with your own issues, share the floor.

5. ***Communicate positively and responsibly.*** Speak from your own experience. Avoid trying to educate or lecture to the other person about their behavior. Use "I" words instead of "You" words when discussing your position. Learn how to express your self in these ways: *"When these kinds of things happen I feel this way."* Or *"I am upset with how you are treating and talking to me."* Avoid saying things such as: *"You are this"* or *"You are that."*

6. ***Try to connect.*** Use collaborative language and try to connect with the other person. Learn to express your self by stating: *"I understand what you are saying and feeling."* And *"Help me to understand what is going on here."* And *"Where do we go from here".* Understanding does not mean that you accept the other person's position, or abuse. It is simply trying to connect with them on a human level. Understanding softens the tensions between you. You can always agree to disagree.

7. ***Walk away.*** If the other person chooses to become or remain angry, hostile, non-communicative or become aggressive, you can choose to say *"I am choosing not to go there with this argument. I'll be ready and willing to talk with you again when there is less tension and emotion."*

8. ***Practice conflict prevention.*** Most arguments and disagreements can be prevented. You minimize conflicts with other people by being respectful of other people's feelings and

rights; by avoiding behavior such as gossip, pettiness and negativity; and by choosing not to allow conflict-oriented people into your circle.

9. ***Own up to your part in bringing about the conflict.*** As hard as it may be, acknowledge what you did to cause any misunderstanding or upset. Don't justify it, 'own' it, and invite the other party to do the same. If they do not, then consider your self the bigger person! In any event, this gesture takes some of the steam out of the conflict.

Always Remember These Basic "Don'ts" When in Conflict

- "You" words puts people on the defensive. Never attempt to speak for other people or chastise them on their behavior.

- Never point your finger at or in someone's face. This is a form of insult, and it will most likely make them defensive.

- Avoid using the word *"But"* when explaining your position, or apologizing, or responding to what the other person is saying. *"But"* takes the positive energy and possibility out of the situation.

- Never, never, never, order the other person to, *"Calm down!"* This will only incite their emotions and the tensions between you, especially when they are very upset.

- Never resort to calling people out of their name or labeling them. That is risky business.

- Try not to turn your back and retreat from a heated exchange that is not resolved. Acknowledge the 'fire' and 'upset' and commit to revisiting the situation later—when it cools.

About the Author

Dr. Elizabeth D. Taylor was born and raised on Chicago's South Side. She moved to San Francisco at age 18 where she attended college and began her lifelong career in personal development and applied spirituality. Elizabeth attended the University of San Francisco, and the Union Institute where she acquired her Masters and Doctoral degrees, respectively.

For 20 years Elizabeth taught at colleges and universities, and consulted to organizations in the areas of business and human growth. Elizabeth's work with youth is extensive, including forums and dialogues for parents and teens across the country. With the 1st Edition of *Straight Up!*, she toured the country, appearing on numerous radio and TV talk shows. She is a media personality, producer and the Founding President of Wisdom To Go, Inc., a not-for-profit organization devoted to human growth and spiritual health.

Dr. Taylor has a teenage son, Julian-Sebastian, and now resides in Phoenix, Arizona.

Tracey Leroy Taylor is a recognized leader and successful Realtor in Chicago, Illinois. He heads up his own firm and mentors teens for the Black Star Project. Tracey was awarded a scholarship from UCLA where he was also a celebrated defensive back for their Bruins. He later graduated from UC Santa Barbara with a degree in Liberal Arts.

Tracey built his real estate business in partnership with his wife, Rutha. As business partners, they also owned and managed a major restaurant franchise. Tracey's real estate talent helped to raise the bar at local Century 21 offices—conceiving $ 1 million in sales for consecutive years. This platform launched his now thriving realty business, which employs a highly skilled team.

Tracey enjoys the exhilaration of competing. He says it lets him know where he stands and where to hit, and the charge of making his mark is gratifying! His volunteer work in the community is extensive, serving as a Director for the Chicago Association of Realtors and its Education Foundation Board. In his work with the Black Star Project Tracey talks with teens about values, focusing and making healthy choices.

Tracey has a young son, Nathanial, who is earning his degree in Business at the University of San Diego.

About Wisdom to Go

Wisdom to Go was founded in 2000 as a not-for-profit organization, devoted to human growth and spiritual health. Self-improvement and spiritual tools are provided to the public via radio broadcasts, media productions, publications, audio/visuals, and learning forums. Since its inception, Wisdom to Go has reached national and international status and impacted thousands of lives. A syndicated talk show, with Dr. Elizabeth Taylor as host, and daily inspirational 'pearls' of wisdom have aired on radio and television since 2000. Straight Up! is a component of Wisdom to Go, Inc., which has served the needs of youths since 1994.

Our website is wisdomtogo.com

ORDER FORM

Wisdom to Go Alliance

Send Checks or Money Orders to:

Wisdom to Go Alliance
P.O. Box 91473
Phoenix, AZ 85066-1473

Please send _____copy(ies) of *Straight Up!* to:

Name:____

Address: ____

City: _____________________________State:_________Zip:__________

Telephone: (_____)_______________________________________

Email:____

I have enclosed $18.95, plus $5.00 shipping per book for a total of $_________.

Sales Tax: Add 7.05% to total book cost for orders shipped to AZ addresses.

For Bulk or Wholesale Rates, call: 602-243-9882 or
Email: etaylor@wisdomtogo.com